The Somerset Village Book

THE VILLAGES OF BRITAIN SERIES

Other counties in this series include

Avon

Bedfordshire

Berkshire

Buckinghamshire

Dorset

Essex

Gloucestershire

Hampshire

Warwickshire

Hertfordshire

Kent

Oxfordshire

Shropshire

Staffordshire

Suffolk

Surrey

East Sussex

West Sussex

Wiltshire

Worcestershire

The Somerset Village Book

Compiled by the Somerset
Federation of Women's Institutes from notes
and illustrations sent by Institutes in the County

Published jointly by
Countryside Books, Newbury
and the SFWI, Taunton

First published 1988

Countryside Books
3 Catherine Road
Newbury, Berkshire

ISBN 1 85306 031 3

Cover photograph of Luccombe by Matthew Stevens

Produced through MRM Associates, Reading
Typeset by Acorn Bookwork, Salisbury
Printed in England by J. W. Arrowsmith Ltd., Bristol

Foreword

A wealth of interest and beauty awaits discovery in the rolling green hills of Somerset. Its coastline stretches from the Mendips to the Quantock Hills with the heights of Exmoor beyond, while to the south lies the lush lowlands with its apple orchards and stately homes.

Amid this setting are the county's many lovely villages, ranging from tiny hamlets of thatched cottages to busy communities with shops, pubs and light industry. Each has its own fascinating story to tell, and almost 200 W.I.s have delved deep to bring them to light.

We thank them all for their help in the creation of this book, and hope they will continue to record all the interesting details of village life for future generations to enjoy.

Diana Chalk
County Chairman

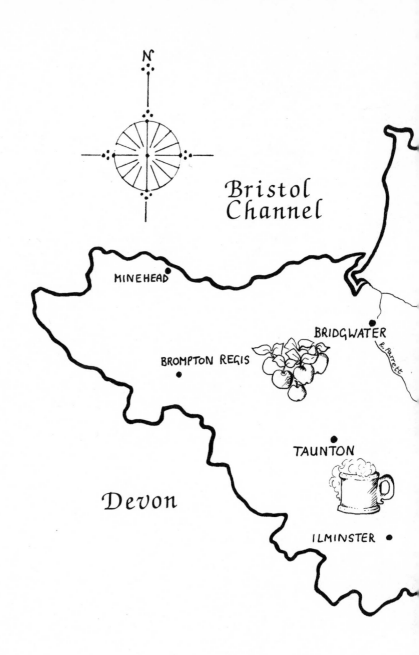

N

Bristol
Channel

MINEHEAD

BRIDGWATER

R.Parrett

BROMPTON REGIS

TAUNTON

Devon

ILMINSTER

Avon

EDDAR

FROME

WELLS

Wiltshire

GLASTONBURY

R. Cary

CASTLE CARY

YEOVIL

Dorset

County of SOMERSET

Acknowledgements

The Somerset Federation of Women's Institutes wish to thank all those members, their families and friends who have worked so hard to research and provide information for this book, and who have provided the excellent drawings.

Also a special thank you to Hilda Treise, the co-ordinator for the project.

Aller

Immortalised in its connection with the illustrious King Alfred, Aller in the name of Kingsalre appears in many documents throughout the centuries.

The village nestles at the foot of the hill – a ridge of woodland, parts of it now conserved as an important example of ancient woodland. To the south west this ancient hill dips to the edge of the green pastures of Sedgemoor. On the warm sheltered slopes, orchids and other wild flowers thrive. The moor has its own wet, succulent beauty divided by willowed banks and rhines.

At one time the local farms were only milk producing but since the moor has been drained, cereals and potatoes are grown as well. Once there was a milk and cheese factory in the village, which when abandoned, gave way to a seed development factory. Years ago there were a few farms and cottages and an inn and manor house with obvious monastic connections (Chantry Farm must have once been a priest's house). Recently the village has been infilled with new houses and bungalows bringing new interests and accomplishments either as hobbies or small businesses to the village.

Aller is well noted for its Pottery, where as far as possible, local materials and colouring are used. Its lovely products are distributed far and wide nationally and internationally.

The Old Pound Inn stands at the fork of the road where the old drove runs westward across the moor and from where there is an old paved path up to the church. The tree in front of the Inn has always been a landmark and a meeting place around which the villagers assemble to dance the New Year in. The old tree has been replaced but its trunk stands nobly in the pub bar. Between the Inn and the Glebe House is the Pound where straying cattle were impounded – probably used often in olden times when the floods meant that animals could swim from one part to another. There are accounts of folk going to church by boats which were also used for carrying corpses for burial.

Looking down from Aller Hill between the tall chimney stacks of the old rectory, a lovely old house still, you can see the church islanded on its Saxon mound and surrounded by trees. This ancient church of St Andrew has a unique place in the history of Britain. It was here in AD 878 that King Alfred stood sponsor at the pagan Danish King Guthrum's baptism in one of the two fonts – both to be seen in the church, one of which was retrieved from the farm pond.

9

Anstey ✤

East and West Anstey are on Exmoor, on the very border with Devon. They consist of a collection of small hamlets, with a total population of 200. The village school has 2 teachers, and about 40 pupils who go on to schools at Minehead, Tiverton and South Molton to continue their education. In addition to the village church there is a Methodist church, a shop, and the Frood Arms public house. A member of the Hancock family who lived here married into the Froods, and there is a stone on Anstey Moor bearing their name. The only industry here is agriculture, but the village has grown and has many retired 'incomers'.

Appley ✤

Appley is a small hamlet situated near the boundaries of Devon and Somerset, with a population of no more than 100.

Most of the industry in the village is farming, comprising two large farms and two smaller ones. There are four council houses and three cottages near the crossroads and a few other cottages scattered at various distances from each other. The old stone school building and the chapel are now converted to private houses.

Several years ago, the village school was threatened with closure but a committee was formed to fight the decision. Eventually the school was reprieved and is now housed in a prefabricated building in the centre of the village, adjacent to the original school building.

Appley itself has no post office or village shop and the nearest post office is at Greenham, some distance away. The Globe Inn still thrives and has been in the ownership of the Enticott family for well over 50 years. The village has a thriving cricket team with their own cricket field and pavilion.

Ash ✤

Ash took a long time to become a community in its own right, having lived under the control of its parent, Martock, ecclesiastically until 1845 and not separated as a civil parish until 1895.

Its original name of 'Esse' first appears in 1225 as a result of the manor of Ash Boulogne being granted to a junior member of the family holding the manorial rights of Martock, only a mile away. The name 'Ash' suggests the presence of ash trees, springing up here like weeds and growing quickly into saplings if left unnoticed.

In the days of compulsory church attendance, villagers had to walk or ride to the Martock church, uphill by the shortest route on the return journey. Flooding caused the lord of the manor of Milton Fauconbridge, a hamlet in the parish, to request a chapel-of-ease in 1287. Now changed to a domestic role, this is the oldest building in the parish.

In 1841, Ash was granted its own chapel-of-ease and a curate, because of the difficulties of getting to Martock. By 1845 he had become the vicar and a fine vicarage was built, now a guest house. A tower with belfry was erected in 1920 by Englands, the village builders. This was conceived as the village peace memorial in thanksgiving, an unusual memorial anywhere.

The school was erected in 1846 by the Church authorities. What was adequate in space then become over-crowded by 1892 when an infants room was added. Mobile classrooms and a staffroom now give good accommodation to local children.

The Bell is one of the oldest buildings in Ash, having begun its life as a barn, combined with Laurel Cottage next door. What were barns of prosperous farmers in times past are now becoming comfortable residences of nonfarmers. The same goes for the substantial farmhouses built of that golden stone quarried from nearby Ham Hill. The 17th century brought prosperity for agriculture and its profits were used in the great rebuilding of their houses by those farmers who were then the controlling influence in the Martock area. No landed estates held sway here.

The presence of pronounced ridges and furrows can be traced in meadows all round the village, silent witnesses to the strip ploughing by oxen in open field times. In Milton Mead small upright stones still indicate a strip system for haymaking. Many field names are still in use, but for how long will they be used with modern farming methods and the disappearance of hedges? The ancients had an imaginative gift for choosing names: Tails, Naps, Lobs, Garry Mead and Hams, whereas we moderns would be stumped for a well-sounding name. 'Fire Beacon' reveals the siting in a field at the highest point in the village of a beacon, one of a chain extending from the coast to points far inland, to warn of the Armada's coming.

Customs come and go, but a special one has been kept up for as long as living memory holds; that of tying the churchyard gates against the approach of the newly-wed couple. Those not in the know have to suffer a delay and further showers of confetti, until a coin is offered as a forfeit.

Ashcott & Pedwell 🐏

The parish of Ashcott, which includes the hamlet of Pedwell, is mentioned in Domesday Book 1086. It was then known as Aissecote and Pedewell, no doubt because of the presence of plentiful spring water. Even today, many of the houses in Pedwell Hill have wells, often unknown to the occupants.

The village is situated on the ridge of the Polden Hills, and is divided by the A39 from Bridgwater and the A361 from Taunton. At their junction stands the Pipers Inn, originally a coaching inn on the Great West Road to London. At one time Queen Isabella of Spain stayed there and scratched her name on a window.

Perhaps the most notable character to be born in Ashcott was Colonel Thomas Pride, who, in 1648, on Cromwell's orders, executed Pride's Purge, excluding from the House of Commons all Presbyterian and Royalist members.

Ashcott has always been mainly a farming community. Some existing families trace their ancestry back to the 17th century. By 1861 there were 817 inhabitants (now about 1300). The village was practically self-sufficient. Ashcott even boasted of a ladies' boarding school! Now there are two shops, a post office, four public houses, a butcher, hairdresser and garage. Basket making and sheepskin retailing are also carried on.

A Stock Fair was held on the Batch every year in January until the First World War. The church car park was the original Pound for stray animals. One man, unwilling to pay for the release of his donkey, climbed into the pound and lifted the animal out.

Ashcott Moor is very much part of the village. For many years the peat, dug by hand, was delivered to villagers for burning on their fires. Today, peat extraction is a thriving industry, and when all of it has been dug out, the sites will become leisure lakes.

Not much can be told of original buildings, as the records, kept in Shapwick Vicarage, were destroyed by fire in 1920. We know that Pedwell Court, built in the 15th century, was used as a Lady Chapel of Glastonbury Abbey. Later it was used as a slaughterhouse, a butcher's and for beer and wine making, finally becoming a farmhouse. Today it is residential. The Manor House in Ashcott, 300 to 400 years old, was divided into two residences in 1911.

The 14th century church of All Saints in Ashcott was described as a handsome stone structure with nave and chancel and a tower containing five bells. After restoration in 1860 and renovation in 1890, it is said to have been spoiled.

The first school was established in 1852 for 125 children, in the old Reading Room, where now sheltered housing has been built. A superb new school was built on the Ridgeway in 1986.

The old schoolroom next to the church was purchased by the village in 1985, together with part of the adjoining glebeland, in order to erect a village hall. Ashcott's first village hall, the Memorial Hall, was built with money collected from villagers in memory of those killed in action in the First World War. Much of the stone came from a local quarry and was donated by farmers. It was sold in 1940, the proceeds being given towards purchasing the Playing Field, still in use today.

The focal point of the village is the Batch, a meeting place for outings and to catch up on local news.

Ash Priors & Halse 🌿

Ash Priors is a small village at the head of the Vale known as Taunton Deane, and the village of Halse adjoins it immediately to the south. The area of Ash Priors was, very recently, 640 acres – one square mile – but is now slightly larger due to boundary adjustments. This makes it one of the smallest of the Taunton Deane parishes but by no means the least. There is now no pub, shop or school, and all that is left is the church and the village hall.

The church of Holy Trinity is of Norman origin, built now entirely in the perpendicular style, much restored in the 1870s under the guise of improvement by the Lethbridge family. In the past they owned most of the parish and lived at Sandhill Park nearby, now a hospital run by the Somerset Health Authority.

Ash Priors is probably best known for its Common, one of the few now left in the Vale. This has been the scene of many quarrels in the past. The most interesting was the attempt by the Lethbridges in 1900 to construct a golf course. They, as Lords of the Manor, owned the Common and under the pretence of providing jobs for the locals in difficult times, started work on the construction. This was bitterly resented by the villagers and culminated in the golf pavilion being pulled over by a team of horses one dark night. The individual concerned was still alive until a few years ago and loved to relate the story.

Ash Priors in medieval times was noted for its bell foundry which was famed over a wide area in the South West. A number of bells cast here are still existing in scattered churches. The actual site of the foundry is not now known, though it is thought to have been either on the Common or on land adjacent. Today, much of the Common is reverting to nature and providing a haven to wildlife and plants, under the auspices of the Somerset Trust for Nature Conservation.

The neighbouring parish of Halse (Saxon for hazel – originally called Halse Priors) is of similar antiquity to Ash Priors and boasts a number of old properties, all now listed, and the village itself is a conservation area. The church of St James the Less dates back to Norman times, and has a particularly fine rood screen. To the north of the parish lies a cluster of buildings known as Stoford where originally was sited a Commandery of the Knights Templar.

Ashwick & Oakhill 🌿

The name Ashwick is of Saxon origin, being variously spelt Aishweeke and Essewiche. It consisted of a green, a pound, a few cottages, dairy farms, a church and Ashwick Court, so called because the Court Leet of the Manor was held there.

The date of the church is unknown but believed to be 14th century. The church was rebuilt in 1825, the galleries removed and the chancel enlarged. Only the tower remains of the original building.

Since the Second World War, the pound and green have disappeared and many houses have been built, including a sports pavilion cum village hall put up by voluntary labour.

Oakhill was a hamlet of a few cottages and farms until 1769, when Mr J Billingsley built Ashwick Grove, and with Mr Jordan founded the Oakhill Brewery. This event turned Oakhill into a village of about 500 inhabitants. Oakhill Stout became very popular, and a small railway line was laid linking the brewery to the nearest station at Binegar. A rather fussy little engine pulled low trucks with barrels of stout across fields, three roads, by two level crossings and a bridge.

Thanks to the brewery, many houses and cottages were built and had the advantage of piped water, sewage and gas long before the turn of the century. The church, Congregational and Methodist chapels were built in the 19th century, also the Church and Chapel schools.

Until the Second World War, Oakhill was a close knit community with people employed at the brewery, farms, mines and quarries.

Since then continuous building has turned Oakhill into a large village, with most people working in surrounding towns. The brewery closed in 1987, the Congregational chapel turned into two houses and there is now only one school, which was enlarged and modernised in 1987.

Barrington ༺

The most famous attraction of this pretty village is undoubtedly Barrington Court. This Hamstone Elizabethan mansion stands surrounded by gardens and parkland, without any outward sign of the turbulent and confused story of its past, linked with both English and international events.

In the Domesday Book it is recorded as part of the Manor of South Petherton; its lords were members of the Daubeny family, some of whom were buried there.

A medieval manor house had stood near the site of the present building but who built the present Court is a mystery. Was it Henry, Earl of Bridgwater, his knowledge of France accounting for the very 'modern' design of a Renaissance home? It is thought that his extravagant life style made this unlikely. William Clifton, a London merchant, was probably the builder.

William Strode bought it in 1625 and built the stable block; the family lived there for more than a hundred years in spite of their anti-Stuart activities. After 1745 there followed a series of absentee owners and the house became known as Court Farm, its Great Hall becoming a cider store.

It was this building, given to the National Trust in 1907 (its first building) which was leased to Colonel A. A. Lyle in 1919. He restored it and created a beautiful garden and a model estate.

The village itself, with its thatched cottages and farmhouses and with St Mary's church set above the road, is also well worth visiting.

Batcombe

From the time men first ventured into the 'combe' to eke out a living from the land the village has prospered. Wool became a means of making money and the clothiers put their money towards the building of the church.

The church stands on a mound in the middle of the village. From its lofty tower the six bells peal out. It was once more ornate than now, and suffered during the Civil War. The rector of that time took a Parliamentary point of view, which did not go down too well with the Royalist views of neighbouring Bruton. In fact an interesting rhyme can be found in the litany of Bruton church dated 1642. It reads thus:

'All praise and thanks to God still give,
For our deliverance Matthias Eve,
By his great power we put to flight
Our raging foes the Batcombites,
Who came to harry, burn and slay
And quite destroy our town this day.'

A shortage of coins during this time prompted a Stephen Parsons to issue his own. He was obviously in the stocking trade because it had a stocking emblem on one side, and 'Batcombe Somerset' on the other. This coin is still in existence.

The village school, built in 1841 by the people of the village raising the money by public subscription, has now closed. But the village hall, again built by money raised by the villagers, is the main venue for most of the social activities held in the village. Of these there are quite a few, because no national event goes by without some sort of celebration. Usually the money raised provides a permanent fixture for the village. On the occasion of King George V's Jubilee, a playing field was established. A beech tree was planted as a memento of the 1937 Coronation. Several trees were planted for the Coronation of our present Queen, and at her Jubilee a seat was provided in the churchyard.

Today life in the village goes on much as before. Many of the old cottages have been renovated, and old barns turned into dwelling houses. The main industry is still agriculture, but a few villagers go outside for their employment.

16

Bawdrip 🐾

Bawdrip is not a pretty name and, to be quite honest, nor is the village. The slow passage of a herd of cows along its roads precludes entry to any 'Best Kept Village' competition, and residents' cars need much cleaning! The name was variously listed in ancient documents as Bakatripe (1166), Baketreppe (1201) and Baggetrippe (1243). Trippe meant 'a trap' and Bagge is supposed to have related to an animal, a small pig, fox or badger. Even today badgers can be seen occasionally in the village.

At its centre, and the centre of much activity, stands the 13th century church which has a central tower of Norman origin and is built to an unusual cruciform plan. The church lays claim to being the place where the bride Eleanor Lovell died. It is said that she hid in an ancient chest during a game on her wedding day but when the lock shut firmly behind her she was imprisoned and not discovered for many years. Other churches claim the legend as theirs but Bawdrip does have a black marble stone behind the altar inscribed in Latin and stating that Eleanor died on June 14th 1681 'taken away by a sudden and untimely fate at the very time of the marriage celebrations'. Her father, Edward Lovell, is listed in the names of rectors (1661).

The church does appear to act as a magnet, the visitors' book revealing the names of people from far and wide. Former residents, war-time evacuees and many who formerly worked in Bawdrip return from time to time to look round the church and its grounds. They can speak of the location of the smithy, the tailor's shop, the sweet shop, all now gone, and the 'Court' where young girls were once 'in service'.

Tudor Court is the other building of great historic interest in the village. Built in 1532 by the Rolle family of Devon, and leased to tenant farmers, it was the former manor house of the village and a court was held there twice a year. Extensions to the house were made in the 17th century and in Victorian times. The original part contains a number of wall paintings, in fact the largest number of 16th century murals in any Somerset house. The present owner, who has treated the property with sensitivity and care, has preserved and treasured a section of glass dating from the time the house was built and strives, without any grant, to conserve the precious murals.

Knowle Hall, a Georgian building, was until quite recently a boys school. It now houses the Institute for Brain Injured Children which receives much support from the local populace.

Berkley 🐚

The parish of Berkley lies to the north-east of Frome, some 4 miles from the town centre. Before 1200 the village was centred on Berkley Marsh, a mile or so from the present 'big house' and church, and boasted a small church, several cottages and 300 or more inhabitants.

Phyl and Flo Chapman, born soon after the turn of the century, have lived in Berkley Marsh for most of their lives. The cottage in which they still live was part of the Mordaunt estate, and their father paid about £70 for it during the First World War. Several of the windows have catches in the shape of a clasped hand, which was a feature of all the buildings on the estate. In those days the baker, Mr Nash, was called the 'Midnight Baker' because he was always late; and besides bread he also made and sold rough cider. The village well, still in existence, supplied water for the surrounding cottages and farms, and villagers walked long distances to obtain it.

Berkley Marsh village and its church have almost disappeared now although there is still a pond near the church site in Pot Lane, which is reputed to have been the village ducking pond. Nowadays Berkley House and the church, both built in about 1750, and the village school form the heart of the hamlet.

There is a strange tale of exorcism in the village. Cissy Watts, a maid at Berkley House, was reputed to be a medium. Strange tappings were heard and her chair would move. Mrs Henderson gave permission for one of the Lavis brothers and two gardeners to sit by Cissy's bedside throughout the night. Cissy was petrified and the tapping was incessant, answering the question, 'What do you want?' with three taps. The men prayed and read passages from the Bible. Finally the tapping stopped and when dawn broke the men were exhausted but Cissy was at peace. She was dismissed from her post and sent home. Ghost stories too prevail. The Rev Crossing lived at the Rectory (now Berkley Grange Nursing Home) and he declared several times that he heard singing in the church late at night. A ghost would be seen coming down the road and would disappear into the cemetery.

Today Berkley has no rectory and no resident rector. There is no wheelwright, although a large garage stands across the road in Standerwick parish. The fete is still held annually in Berkley House with the proceeds going towards the upkeep of the church. The Cricket Club still thrives and the village school has 70 or so pupils although several years ago it was threatened with closure through lack of children. Deer still roam the woods around the Chapmans' cottage and Turner's Farm; surely all the wild life will feel the impact when the Frome by-pass comes across the fields in one or two year's time.

Moors Farm has been sold to a firm of Auctioneers and Estate Agents and is to be the new site for Frome Cattle Market. The market will be moving out of Frome after being held in the town for some 800 years and this is bound to make a difference to Berkley.

Berrow 🌿

Once a small village, Berrow has grown tremendously in the last 20 years with many people retiring here. It boasts a first class golf course and a 13th century church, as well as a 100 year old Welsh-type pig-sty preserved as an agricultural by-gone!

On the beach are the remains of a Norwegian ship, the *Nornen* which ran aground in 1897, the figurehead from which was given to a local resident by the Captain. Withy Cottage was one of the oldest fishermen's cottages in the village and was the holiday home of Ben Travers, the author and playwright.

The sand dunes offer some very rare species of orchid and marsh hellebore as well as some unusual bird life.

Bicknoller 🌿

Bicknoller lies at the foot of the Quantock Hills. Men have lived here for centuries working the fields and rearing their families on the produce of the land. The earliest inhabitants probably lived in Trendle Ring, the old camp on the slopes of the hills. The name Bicknoller has two possible derivations: 'Bica's Alder', a Saxon name, or 'Bychan' – small and 'Alwar' – treasury, two ancient words.

From the tower of the 15th century church of St George grotesque but worn gargoyles poke out their heads. The art of local medieval craftsmen can be seen in the early Tudor carving of the chancel screen and pew ends, and in the sculpture on the pillar capitals. Of interest are the original stone altar and the 15th century stone font. There are four bells in the tower, one of them pre-Reformation (1420–60). The bells and their ringers were the subject of a little rhyme made long ago by the ringers themselves:

'One, two, dree, vower,
Vower vools in Bicknoller Tower'

In the churchyard the ancient stocks shelter beneath a large split yew tree, near the old stone cross. A row of seven tombstones is all that remains of the Bickham family who entertained large numbers of guests to champagne breakfasts, followed by organised coursing with their greyhounds. If the direction of the wind was wrong for hunting, they shot at the weathercock on the church tower and the holes can still be seen. At the top of the churchyard by the wrought iron gate commemorating the reign of Queen Victoria, is the village pound where straying animals were kept until claimed by their owners.

Church registers, started in 1557, provide information about the people of the village. Few of these names still survive but many of the old houses are called by the names of their original owners – Gatchells, Ford, Locks, Dashwoods. Bicknoller was a farming community, farmers having Commoners' Rights to graze as many sheep on the hills in summer as they could keep on their turnips in winter.

A school was built on the village green in 1863 but closed through lack of pupils in 1912. Village activities took place in the schoolroom until 1954 when a hall was built on donated land nearby, the cost being met from fund-raising efforts. This attractive hall, together with the church, form the centre for all the events and activities which maintain the character and community spirit of a living village.

Binegar

Binegar is a small village on the Mendips, 600 to 700 feet above sea level. The name of the village is of Saxon origin and was first recorded in 1065 as Beazenhangra, the best translation of which is 'Slope where the beans grow'.

All that remains of the 14th century Holy Trinity church is the tower. The nave and chancel were rebuilt in the mid 19th century. There is a stone carving representing the Trinity on the tower which is reputed to be one of the best examples in the county.

Binegar school was opened in 1862 with 20 pupils of all ages. The first qualified head teacher was appointed in 1874 and served in the post for

41 years. In 1930 it became a Primary School and the buildings have been extended several times since it was first built. There are now about 55 children on the roll.

Most of the land surrounding the village is given over to dairy farming and several farmers are now rearing more sheep. Although quarrying was once quite extensive in the village, there is at present only one quarry operating, supplying stone for road-making and crushed stone for making cement.

Binegar was an important station on the Somerset and Dorset railway from Bath to Bournemouth. Products from the Oakhill Brewery and the local quarries and coal mines were carried from the station to many destinations. The line closed in 1966. All that remains is the station house and the yard which is used as a coal depot. Now the only public transport serving the village is the bus service from Bath to Wells.

For recreational and cultural activities in the village there is the Memorial Hall and the recently acquired well-equipped children's playing field.

Binegar Fair, held in the field adjacent to the church during Whit week until 1955 was a well known horse fair, possibly moved from Wells at the time of the Black Death. Horses were brought from far and wide to be sold here, and many tales were told of fighting and brawling among gypsies and others around the village.

Private Henry Martin, one of the defenders of Rorke's Drift during the Zulu war, lived in the village until his death in 1937. His grave can be seen in the churchyard.

Bishop's Hull 🌿

Bishop's Hull, grown from a population of 683 in 1801 to over 3000 in 1988, is a village struggling to keep its identity, and so far succeeding. Probably older than Taunton, it stands on a ridge nearly two miles west of the town. The Bishop of Winchester's purchase of the manor of Taunton in AD 904 explains the name's earlier form, 'Hyllebishops', the hill belonging to the Bishop, who still owns the mineral rights.

From 1120 the church belonged to Taunton Priory. Both were dedicated to St Peter and Paul. Medieval rebuilding added the Lady Chapel and an octagonal tower in the shape of a weaver's beam, said to be the gift of cloth-workers. There are good 16th century bench ends. Some box

21

pews are numbered or marked 'free', reminders of the system of paying pew-rent, and have holes for sprigs of Christmas holly.

The Manor or Great House was built about 1530 by Simon Farwell, who came from Yorkshire. Like many large old houses, it is to be part of a nursing home complex, so will be preserved.

A school at the bottom of Shutewater Hill preceded the Board School of 1893, itself superseded by the new combined Primary School and Community Centre opened in September 1978, now with 294 pupils.

Mr Bond, a local businessman who lost his only son in the last war, left land and money to help the elderly. The Frank Bond Centre is a social club in his former home. St Margaret's Somerset Hospice, with 16 beds, and the Abbeyfield Extra-Care House with 21, both opened in 1987, owe much to his generosity.

Gone are the cobb cottages opposite Haydon House, where within living memory one stout lady sat outside pressing her husband's shirts by sitting on them. Carts no longer follow the old main road to the west through the village carrying criminals to be hanged at the gallows by Stone hamlet – Stone Gallows. The first recorded executions were in 1624, when three men and a woman were hanged for the murder of the curate of Old Cleeve, and the last in 1810.

Bishopswood 🌿

The wood, recently cut down, was called 'Big Wood' by the old people who remembered going there as youngsters to collect sweet chestnuts. It was the Bishop of Winchester to whom Queen Frithogyth, in about AD 730, gave a large grant of land near Taunton, although many think that the village was among smaller parcels of land added to the grant later.

Looking at a map of early this century, one could have seen why the village had a reputation for independence, for practically every one of the few old cottages and the more modern little flintstone houses had their own two or three small fields, perhaps an orchard, to keep a bullock or two, and pigs to sell at the local Fairs. Thus there was no 'Master and Man' relationship between the villagers of Bishopswood and the small family-size farms that make the parish of Otterford, but they gave part-time help at haymaking, harvest and threshing. They may also have helped at the lime kilns which were working here from 1861 to 1894 when they closed.

The church of St Leonard's, Otterford, is not in the village, but 'out in the blue'! Old English, with a Norman font, it was a pilgrim church, so called, on the way from Exeter to Glastonbury. Two monks at Church Farm gave 'bed and breakfast', and no doubt enjoyed the news and gossip from either direction.

A chapel in the village was once used also as a school, to which the children walked in all weathers.

Perhaps a mile out, there are two listed buildings. The first, Lower Whatley, said to be 14th century, a yeoman-farmer's home, is well kept and almost unspoilt. A little further on is Otterford Mill, called in a Saxon charter at the end of the 10th century, Whatley Mill. It still has practically all the machinery and was working for some time after the Second World War, but the flood of 1968 washed away the weir further up the river and the leat is now dry.

Climate? We run from about 350 feet where the village starts with a bridge over the Yarty, to nearly 800 at the top, as they say 'an overcoat different' to the people 'down below'. Our winters have been very severe, but now are milder and much wetter, thanks, we are told, to the pollution in the atmosphere nowadays. Dairy farmers here will be thankful it is not snow, remembering the blocked lanes and deep drifts through which they had to take the milk churns to some spot on the main road along the top of Brown Down from which a milk lorry would collect them – if possible. And the gorgeous view across the valley to the long hill of Buckland St Mary with its beech-clump that can be seen for miles around, did not make up for the miserable cold of it all.

Blagdon Hill 🐝

Blagdon Hill is a typical Somerset village, in that it meanders along both sides of a long, winding road. This road is the old turnpike from Taunton, four miles to the north, that carried the coaches over the Blackdown Hills to Devon and beyond. It is easy to see how the village got its name – and it does need the word 'Hill', to distinguish it from Blagdon on the Mendips. More than one lorry-driver has turned nasty when told he has another 50 miles to go.

There is one shop/post office, a large garage and two good pubs, the White Lion and the Lamb and Flag, but no church. This is a mile away over the fields or down the lane to Pitminster, the original settlement of the parish, mentioned in Domesday and known to have had a church in

AD 938, over a thousand years ago. The earliest mention of Blagdon Hill in the records is around 1225.

Blagdon Green, a triangular field at the top of the village, was anciently the site of the pound, where straying cattle were penned, and the parish saw-pit operated there in the 18th century. The Green was enclosed and sold in 1851, but was still to be regarded as 'a place of Exercise and Recreation for the Inhabitants'. The Mission Room on the corner of the Green, was erected for the benefit of parishioners living right up the hill. It is now a furniture store, but there is still a right of way across the Green and a memorial tree planted by the Parish Council to replace the dead Jubilee Oak of 1935.

Nearer to Taunton is the Memorial Playing Field at Sellicks Green, some 4½ acres bought in 1950 with the Welcome Home Fund collected after the Second World War. It has given much pleasure since then and is the scene of the Annual Fete in June. Here is also a really unique feature – a re-erected Bronze Age standing stone, found nearby during rescue archaeology work on the motorway. The Member of Parliament, then Mr Edward du Cann, poured a libation of cider over it at the unveiling ceremony in July, 1982.

There are other traces of the past, but the tannery down Curdleigh Lane and the nearby malthouse are now part of private premises and the old farrier's forge has been converted to a modern metal-working shop.

Newer houses and bungalows fill almost every space left by the few old cottages and farmhouses, and the great elms have all gone, but the country on either side is still lovely and unspoiled at all seasons, under the wooded hills above.

Bradford on Tone ✑

Bradford is an ancient village, originally a Saxon 'broad ford' across the river Tone. Many people have come here over the centuries, including Viking raiders!

The Normans built the church of St Giles, which was substantially altered between the late 14th and early 16th centuries. Sir John de Meriet, whose effigy lies in the church, was instrumental in beginning the work.

The wool trade brought prosperity to the village and there was once a project to join Exeter and the Severn by a Grand Canal. Unfortunately money was short and nothing came of it.

In the 19th century Bishop Wilkinson of the Court, had the Black Boy Inn pulled down and built the villagers a club room instead. The Poor House is gone now and the chapel is a private home. The school, thriving until 1984, is now joined with Oake, the next village. St Katherine's school for girls and St George's for boys were schools full of character, but have now made way for modern flats.

Now most villagers commute to Taunton and new houses have changed the face of Bradford. Some of the old village names still survive though and members of old families still sit in the church pews as their ancestors did before them.

Brean 🦯

With the growth of the holiday industry, Brean loses its small rural community in the summer months. By September there are many signs of the village settling into winter activities. Several organizations use the village hall, built in 1977 on Church Trust property. Unfortunately there is no longer a school, it having closed in 1933.

You may be held up on the winding narrow lanes by a herd of cows, which is a sign that a thriving dairy farming community still exists today. The village farmers no longer produce Caerphilly Cheese. So excellent was the cheese that Highbridge market in the 1920s and 1930s attracted Welsh traders, who in turn sold the product to the mining towns of South Wales.

The footpaths along the top of Brean Down make a really enjoyable walk anytime of the year. It is now part of the National Trust, but as you will see, it has been part of the military establishment for three periods of history at least – the Napoleonic and those of the First and Second World Wars.

The Celtic word for hill, Bryn, gives Brean its name. The church of St Bridget has a Celtic foundation, according to legend. In the churchyard an Iron Heart bears the inscription:

> 'The cruel winds and yawning waves
> hurried me to my doom,
> While wife and children dear
> waited at home.'

This memorial marks the graves of sailors washed up on the beach. Prior to 1880 their remains were buried on the seashore, above high-water

25

mark. In the glebe field next to the churchyard are the remains of a haybarn which served as a mortuary for the drowned sailors, the inquests being held at the Old Rectory.

In 1988, the Methodist church and the church of St Bridget signed a covenant making Brean the first local ecumenical project in Somerset. Regular worship is held in each church with United services at least once a month.

In 1988 Mercury Communications, a member of the Cable and Wireless Worldwide Communications, will provide an optical cable across the Atlantic to North America, starting from Brean. The future plans may well include satellite dishes. What a far cry from the days of Marconi, who sent one of his first messages from the top of Brean Down.

Brent Knoll

Brent Knoll is an enigma. How else can one describe this hill of 450 feet that appears to rise suddenly out of the Somerset Levels. It is said that this 'nob' of lias rock came into being as the Devil excavated Cheddar Gorge and threw his shovelfuls of earth on to this flat land! More likely is the fact that millions of years ago, the Knoll would have been surrounded by sea and as the water subsided so this rock surveyed a scene of marshland – hence, the Romans later named it 'Frog Island'.

The hilltop, now belonging to The National Trust, was originally an Iron Age hill fort and later a place of safety for the Saxons when the warring Danes fought their last battle in this area, at the base of the Knoll, known as 'Battleborough' in AD 875.

But what of the village itself? Until the Great Western Railway passed this way in the 1880s, the village was known as South Brent but, causing postal confusion with South Brent in Devon, it was decided that it should take the name of the ancient hill and be known as Brent Knoll.

Over the past two hundred years, the population has trebled to approximately 1200 people with many more houses being build – but fewer people finding their occupations locally. In the past thirty years, small groups of houses have sprung up and much infilling of green spaces has caused heartache amongst those remembering the gracious housing of the past. It is to be expected that Brent Knoll might become more of a dormitory village, and, in some ways it has, but it is also very much alive.

The two churches, St Michael's, which has witnessed village events since Norman times, and the Methodist church which was built by the

Bible Christians 150 years ago, have had a lot to offer the parishioners in spiritual guidance and social activities and still do.

The craftsmen of the Middle Ages left their mark in St Michael's church by carving a beautiful ceiling over the north aisle and three of the bench ends depict a 'cartoon' to show the displeasure that the Abbot of Glastonbury caused the priest and parishioners of the village by wanting to seize some parish revenue. He was depicted as a wily fox, defrocked and placed in the stocks, then later hanged!

Brent Knoll may not be blessed with many outstanding pieces of architecture, but it has several interesting houses dating roughly from the 17th century onwards. One or two older houses survived the floods of 1607 and there are some fine Georgian country houses to be seen. Builders were busy in Victorian times, but of the new buildings, little has been designed to carry on local tradition. As dairy farming has been the main industry for centuries, one or two families have roots long established in the village – a tradition of which to be proud.

The oldest inhabitant staying at Holywell, the Nursing Home in the village, is in her 106th year, and must look back in amazement at the changes that have occurred during her lifetime. The younger people must wonder what the future has in store!

Brewham 🐾

First came the river Brue – the Saxon 'bru' meant wild and violent. 'Bru-haem' was probably a fenced off part of the Bruton domain. The river rises from a little spring in Kingsettle Woods, marked by a simple grotto whose stones bear the initials of Henry Hoare, a member of the great banking family, who owned great estates in the area including most of Brewham. As you follow the little trickle of water down the hill and through the fields to the centre of Brewham, you cannot imagine where the description of 'violent' originated. But do not be fooled – a flood alleviation scheme is under way. The river divides North Brewham and South Brewham – nothing else does, we are a very united village.

The church is dedicated to St John the Baptist, and is recorded as having three services a week in 1180, served by clergy from Bruton Priory. Little if any of the original building remains but there is evidence of 13th century work in the tower, the churchyard cross and the remains of an even earlier font in the church are not easy to date. The church has the oldest signed brasses in Somerset, by Cockey, bell-founders and metal workers of Wincanton and excellent 15th century roof-timbers and bosses.

Sixty years ago, or so, the Wesleyan church in North Brewham flourished, in addition to St John's and the Baptist Chapel, and many people remember a strong sect of 'Gillites', who came from miles around to Goodedge Farm. They erected a marquee and spent several days singing and praying and carrying out full white-robed, total immersion baptisms in a local, none too clean, stream. They also held 'Irish wakes' type burial services and buried their dead in unmarked graves in the parish burial ground.

Farming and forestry have been the main sources of employment in the area for centuries. In earlier centuries farming was mainly sheep rearing and the forestry the maintenance of broad-leaved areas for royal hunting. Today farms are mostly given over to dairy farming and the woodlands are managed and mostly conifers. There are two flourishing horse-breeding studs in the area.

The village still has a post office, the bakery and stores producing the best bread in the county and delivering it to villages all around. The 350 voters on the Register of Electors have a choice of three good pubs! Sadly the village school has gone but it is now the village hall and has just undergone a complete overhaul, after the local people have made stupendous efforts of fund-raising.

Brompton Ralph

It is commonly supposed that the village name was derived from the broom plant which is a feature of the hillsides in spring, but further research implies that the name Brompton is a corruption of Brendon because the village nestles in the southern slopes of the Brendon Hills. The suffix 'Ralph' came from its lord, Ralph son of William, in the 12th century.

The village consists of a scatter of cottages and farms of various dates around two village greens. The larger Brompton Green lies beside the church and was allotted for recreation in 1845. The smaller was formerly the pound and nowadays flanks the Post Office Stores. Perhaps it still has an atmophere of refuge because it so often happens that on this triangle of grass where three lanes converge, straying animals pause for a nibble enabling the postmistress to telephone their probable owners.

John Toms, glass stainer, was born in Brompton Ralph between 1813 and 1815 and his work can be seen in several nearby churches. In 1913 a Mr Toms, his descendant, came from the USA and paid for the restoration of the ancient screen in the church in his memory.

Probably the most interesting surviving building in the village is a cottage which seems to have been a parsonage or church house. The present owner has uncovered beneath layers of plaster on a sitting room wall a painting of religious theme. The lack of perspective and the figures' neck ruffs and little pointed toes imply an early Renaissance period of origin although so far nobody has established records of any authorship or history.

In the 1970s when the village hall was recreated from the remains of the old Sunday Schoolhouse a few enthusiastic members of an art class painted a mural of the life of the village with several recognisable characters including the then rector on his motorbike. The village is as proud of this work of art as of its 16th century predecessor.

The village has no pub and has long lost its school and its bus service but is fortunate in its well stocked shop. Who could possibly prefer a supermarket? And when, as occasionally happens, the lanes to Wiveliscombe are blocked with snow, nobody starves.

As in olden times agriculture and sheep are the daily labour of the inhabitants, who are a happy mixture of the old families and newcomers and who keep alive old crafts (the archway curtains in the church are handspun and handwoven) and collaborate in the seasonal activities of the church and the non-conformist chapel.

Brompton Regis

Brompton Regis is on Exmoor. The 13th century church of St Mary faces Haddon Hill, and contains a brass to a member of the Dykes family, who died in Stuart times:

> Reader, it is worth thy pains to know,
> Who was interred here below,
> Here lies good nature, pity, wit,
> Though small in volume, yet most fairly writ.
> She died young, and so oft-times tis seen,
> The fruit God loves, He's pleased to pluck it green.

Brushford 🌿

Wooded river valleys and undulating green hills rising to 800 feet create the visitor's first impression of Brushford parish. It lies on the southern edge of the Exmoor National Park, and its bounds include the rivers Barle and Exe, with the Brockey which gives the village its name.

In the old days the farms were self-sufficient, growing corn and potatoes and keeping pigs, poultry, sheep and cattle, Red Devon being the local breed of cattle and Devon Closewool or Devon Longwool the sheep. The farmers' staple diet was fat pork, potatoes and cider – the

Brushford village, with its Parish Church of St Nicholas

30

village was full of orchards and 'scrumpy' was made on many farms and was even drunk by children. The pigs were grown very big and when cut showed more fat than lean. There were competitions to see which housewife made the best lard.

The coming of the railway revolutionised Brushford, bringing new forms of employment and new housing half a mile from the old village.

A cattle market was held monthly, by Messrs Phillips, for over 100 years. The breeding and store stock were sold where Market Close now stands and the fat stock adjoining the Corn Mill. There were cattle holding pens in the station yard and large numbers of cattle were driven by horse riders 'rodeo fashion' from Cutcombe and Exford down the Exe valley to be loaded on to special wagons.

The mid-1930s saw a new kind of development, the building of Council houses on land north of the new road, with a further wave after the war, making Brushford a 'working' village not a picture-postcard one, which is part of its character.

The service industries allied to tourism provide most employment. Some commute to the factories in Tiverton but agriculture is in decline, small farmers work their own land and employ casual labour. There are several self-employed labourers in the village.

In 1921 a First World War hospital hut from Minehead was re-erected in the village as a parish room, and it still hosts activities from dog classes to dancing, and playgroup to Women's Institute. St Nicholas church still flourishes, with its Norman font and parish chest, rood screen, early 16th century stained glass as well as an 1891 window by William Morris's firm.

Buckland Dinham ☙

Buckland Dinham lies amid undulating landscape near Orchardleigh woods, three miles from Frome on the A362, with some 125 houses.

Dinham was derived from the aristocratic Dinan family and the Norman style church was given in the 12th century by Oliver de Dinan. Across the road from the attractive lychgate stands a guard house or 'blind house' with tiny barred porthole window, at one time the lockup for disorderly people!

In the 15th century the manufacture of cloth brought prosperity to the village; teasles were grown to dress the cloth. Still in existence is a packhorse bridge and dyehouse remains. Numerous pedlars converged

31

upon an ancient weekly market and annual three-day Michaelmas fair. A part of the old market cross stands at present in the churchyard.

Games of fives were played on the north side of the church tower until a complaint was made at Taunton sessions, due to damage to the church wall and windows! Shrove Tuesday's contest was 'cock-throwing', when a bird in an earthen vessel, 'head and tail' exposed, was strung up across the street a few feet off the ground and thrown at! Whoever broke the pot and freed the bird took him for his prize.

At Fairfield there was once a turnpike, coal frequently being carted through the village. In 1830 people drew these trucks, and often children not more than 9 years of age. Another venture was Buckland Coal Syndicate, with the boring of a hole some 896 feet deep; this enterprise failed due to continuous flooding by water below ground, the chimney still stands aloft as evidence.

Buckland Dinham has one public house, one chapel, one church and a car repairs/sales service. Unfortunately the post office stores has closed. The school, old parsonage, old vicarage and new vicarage are private residences. A vicar centred at Mells cares for 5 parishes. Seven dwelling-houses now sit on Court Orchard green.

Village characters are fondly remembered, like Bob Brown, a road-mender, whose clothes were always on the large side and who tied his baggy corduroy trousers with twine under his knees. One day about to go home, he asked his workmates, 'Yer, 'ave any on ee sid me westcot?' (waistcoat). After looking round the reply came, 'Theise got un on Bob!' 'Zo I 'ave,' Bob said, 'Good job theise told I or I zhould 'ave gone 'ome be-out un!'

Buckland St Mary 🌿

Partly inside the parish of Buckland St Mary on the Blackdown Hills, and dominating the landscape, is Castle Neroche. Considered to be an Iron Age fort, the massive concentric earthworks are now tree-grown, and have been for ages past. The land is managed by the Forestry Commission and affords exciting nature trails open to the public.

There is a legend of two giants quarrelling; one lobbed a huge boulder from a vantage point on the earthen ramparts and it remains where it came to rest, at the side of the road to Staple Fitzpaine – a Sarson Stone. Other legends claim it as the work of the Devil and hint that it will bleed if pricked at certain times of the year. In Somerset unusual geological formations are frequently described in legends as the work of giants or the Devil.

George Brealey who, supported by the Quaker families of Fox and Hanbury, started the Blackdown Mission in 1863 or 1864, said that the beauty of the countryside contrasted sharply with the moral degradation and gross superstitions in which most of the Blackdowners were steeped. He found great poverty due to unemployment and sickness as well as ignorance.

Later in the last century, Buckland, a small scattered, hill-farming community must have been almost self-sufficient. Quite recent records tell of a bakery, two blacksmiths, a butcher, wheelwright, boot repairer and a tailor, shop and post office. Farmers made their own cider and housewives their home-made wine. Until World War Two the water mill was used for grinding cattle food. The mill remains and the notice on it may still be deciphered:

'If you want cake, corn or meal
Come to Jenkins at the Mill,
And all kinds of poultry food
Prices are right and quality good,
So send a card to him to-day
You'll be supplied without delay.'

For other commodities the villagers had to send to Taunton or Chard. If they could not go themselves a local businessman with a pony and trap would fetch things for a small fee. Alternately they could wait until the last Tuesday of September for Buckland's own Annual Fair.

Until 1830 various curates maintained the church services, then the patrons – the Pophams of Littlecote, presented the Rev John Lance, and the wealthy Lance dynasty of three generations tidied up everything they could lay their hands on. First John Lance built a Victorian Gothic mansion for himself – 'A house fit to live in' – now Buckland House. Next he replaced the 15th century church with one of the 'Middle Pointed' Gothic style, so large that it rightly earned the title of the Cathedral of the Hills. They piped an existing water supply into a picturesque edifice known as the fountain, and Buckland must have been one of the few small Somerset villages to boast a cobbled main street. The large church and the influence the Lance family exercised remain as their memorial.

Burrowbridge 🌿

Burrow Bridge has a great deal of history attached to it, for it was here in the year AD 878 King Alfred took shelter to plan his battle with the Danes, who were later defeated. In thankfulness for this victory he built an abbey on rising ground, as most of the land on the level was a swamp. No trace of the abbey has been found in recent years apart from stones brought to the surface when ploughing, also some bits of tiles. An obelisk marks the spot of the abbey. A short distance away is another church built on a hill, known locally as the 'Mump'. It may have guarded Alfred's headquarters. This church was dedicated to St Michael and during excavations in 1939 the skeleton of a young man was found with a bullet in his shoulder – he may have been killed fighting in the battle for Langport in 1645.

Most of the houses were built on the river bank as bricks were available from the brickyards in Bridgwater and were brought up the river by barge.

Eventually the railway line was built and Burrow Bridge provided with a small station, as well as a little motor train. For 6d you could travel to Langport and 1/- for Taunton – all together in one long coach so one could hear everything that had happened over the week! In later years the London trains passed through – shrieking and echoing across the moors especially when the floods were up.

Burrow Bridge also had a yearly fair which was held in the yard of the King Alfred Inn, next to the vicarage – it consisted of one stall loaded up with sweets of every description and bag upon bag of Betty's gingerbread!

Every villager worked hard – either managing willows or keeping a few cows and the usual pig for winter meat, as well as a few fowls. Everyone made cider from the few apple trees on most properties so one always had some callers. Some of the cows used to graze on the river bank as there was always plenty of grass.

Butleigh 🌿

Spelt in as many different ways as most place names on old documents are, Buddekaulegh (meaning Budeca's Leigh or Field) is first recorded in AD 821 when King Egbert of the West Saxons made a gift to his servant Edgils, of 80 measures of land.

Butleigh has had a succession of Lords of the Manor at Butleigh Court. The Grenvilles became Lords of the Manor in 1738, and in the following years a new house was built taking land from the churchyard and causing a legend to grow that because bones had been disturbed, the house would go within a hundred years. The family have gone, but the Court has been restored and now houses four families.

Robert Neville Grenville, the last Squire of Butleigh, was a memorable Somerset man who was educated at Eton and Cambridge and was a skilled engineer. He not only drove a railway engine, but had one named after him, *The Butleigh Court*. In 1875 he designed and built the Grenville Steam Carriage, believed to be the world's oldest self-propelled passenger-carrying road vehicle. It was used as a road vehicle, and later as a stationary engine to work a cider press. Now it is a prize exhibit at the Industrial Museum in Bristol, and is still brought into use in ever-popular Steam Rallies.

The Long Ashton National Fruit and Cider Institute owes much of its pioneer work to research done by Robert Neville Grenville in his cider house at Butleigh.

The vicars of Butleigh have also left reminders of their names; Higher Rocke and Lower Rocke farmhouses relate to the Rev Thomas Rocke who was vicar in 1577. Sadly, they are no longer working farms. The Rev Samuel Hood, who was made vicar in 1723 and lived at the Old Vicarage (now Butleigh House), was the father of two famous sons, Admiral Lord Hood and Lord Bridport. Admiral Sir Samuel Hood was a grandson of Rev Samuel's older brother and is commemorated by the monument on the Poldens, south west of the village.

Butleigh today has a very different role from the old manorial one. The houses are privately owned, there are two small estates, and only two of the farms and smallholdings remain as working units, the rest are private dwellings.

The school still functions, there is a village post office/store which also sells newspapers, a butcher's shop and a pub. The village has many organisations centred round the school and the church room.

Cannington ✤

The village of Cannington lies on the A38 road from Bridgwater to Minehead, and has grown into an extremely busy and important village. It evolved from a settlement, the home of the Cangii, a tribe of Ancient Britons.

Above the village on a hill to the north west is what is now called Cannington Park, the site of an Iron Age Hill Fort which over the years has been commercially quarried by a local firm. In 1962–3 an interesting excavation revealed about 400 graves containing perfectly preserved skeletons. This was a truly remarkable sight. The graves had been literally hewn out of the rock face. This site was thought to be part of a much larger burial ground of as many as 5,000 graves. The area of the burial ground is thought to have been occupied from the Neolithic & Beaker period, right through to Medieval times.

Among several historical houses in Cannington, at least two are worth a special mention, they are Blackmore House, mentioned in the Domesday Survey of AD 1085, this house contains a chapel and a priest's chamber, it is now the home of a local farmer. The other is Gurney Manor an excellent example of an Elizabethan Manor.

In the fine church of St Mary the Virgin, the tower is 14th century while the interior of the tower and bells were renovated in 1900. There are still some stones from the original Norman church to be seen.

Brymore Secondary Technical School of Agriculture for boys of 13 and over, the only school of its kind in the country, is housed in Brymore House on the outskirts of the village. This house was the birthplace of John Pym, the 17th century politician.

Cannington College of Agriculture and Horticulture has grown tremendously with many new buildings and halls of residence, it was originally Cannington Farm Institute and was partly housed, and still is, in the Old Priory adjacent to the parish church. This priory was once the home of an order of Benedictine nuns until it was closed in 1536. Legend tells that the Fair Rosamund, loved by Henry II, was born at the priory and spent part of her childhood in the nunnery.

The village has changed dramatically since 1957 when work commenced on the construction of the Hinkley Point Nuclear Power Station. The road from Cannington to Combwich and Stogursey was merely a country lane until the construction gangs moved in and carved a new road to the power station. The influx of workers necessitated the building of many new houses when the population greatly increased.

Another unusual feature of the village is the fact that there are three bridges over the brook, the original Pack-Horse Bridge, still intact, the Old Road Bridge and the A39 road bridge, the fourth means of crossing the brook was a ford which has only recently disappeared. It is thought that four crossings together like this is unique.

Chapel Allerton 🪶

The parish of Chapel Allerton includes the hamlets of Ashton and Stone Allerton. It lies on the south-west side of the low ridge known as the Isle of Wedmore. The population at the 1981 census was 313. Allerton was mentioned in Domesday as Alwarditone.

The church dates from the 13th century but was extensively rebuilt and enlarged in the 19th century. The mounting block outside the gate is part of the ancient hundred stone which once stood in the hundred stone field, marking the boundary of the Bempstone Hundred.

The village boasts one of only two remaining windmills in Somerset with sails. The first mention of a mill was in 1317. The present building dates to about 1760 and was last used in 1927, the last mill to be used in Somerset. The workings are almost complete and there are plans to renovate the cap and enable the sails to be canvassed and turned. The cap would be thatched as it was originally. The mill now belongs to Sedgemoor District Council and a team of volunteers opens it to the public on Sunday afternoon.

Farming was the main occupation and 35 years ago there would have been approximately 30 farms, today there are 7. Traditionally the farms had some land on the higher ground and summer pasture on the moor. The milking bail was a feature of this part of Somerset – a portable milking cabin taken down to the cows in summer – but this is seen much less frequently. Milk is still the main commodity and is collected by tankers for the Milk Marketing Board. In recent years sheep have become much more important and lambs appear from Christmas onwards. Formerly there were many orchards and most farms made cider but only for their own use, and the cider house was a favoured meeting place. Now, although made nearby, none is made in the village. Cheese was also an important part of the economy. Cheddar and Caerphilly were produced. The latter was sent to South Wales by train from Highbridge.

Today there are a few more houses but smaller households. Many people are self-employed and work in the surrounding villages or from home. A number commute to Bristol, Weston and Bridgwater.

The Harvest Home, a unique feature in this part of Somerset, takes place in September. Fund raising events for the Church are numerous.

Riding is a popular pursuit and the village pub, The Wheatsheaf, together with the church, the hall and the shop (just one) continue to be the main meeting places in the village.

Charlton Horethorne

This small village is situated on the B3145 midway between Wincanton and Sherborne on the southern boundaries of the County, with an increasing population of around 450.

The village is purported to derive its name from a thorn tree which stood on the spot where the Hundred Courts were held in ancient times. This was probably Poyntington Down, on the borders of Charlton and Poyntington parishes.

The main feature of this sprawling village is the church of St Peter and Paul which occupies an elevated position on the main road approached from a path through lychgates. The interior, although much renovated, has a very pleasing appearance with several outstanding features. The building dates from the 13th century whilst the north aisle in the decorated style is rather later. In the 15th century, the chancel was enlarged and the tower added. At right angles to the church is the manor house.

The main water supply used to be from the conduit, and people nearby used their yokes and buckets to collect their daily supply. Horse-drawn water carts backed between the pond and the conduit to fill up for farm supplies. A long pipe from the conduit fitted into the top of the water cart for 'filling'. This pipe vanished long ago. Later, tap houses were put at a number of places in the village and people would carry their water home from the nearest 'house'. One is opposite the school.

Charlton Feast was held on or near the 29th June and it was a great festive occasion. Stalls of all kinds lined the street and the village green, and celebrations continued late into the night. This event has recently been resurrected and is celebrated in the village on the last Saturday in June. All the villagers are encouraged to take part by dressing up in period costume.

One of the old traditions which no longer exists was a party for all the villagers held on Christmas Eve. Just before 12 when the church bells chimed, everyone trooped along to the church for midnight mass. There is one tradition still maintained which is the distribution of bread to the poor and needy. A notice displayed in the village shop announces the time when the vicar will hand out loaves.

The village is the home of the Blackmore Vale Hunt and this colourful spectacle attracts many people to its various meets throughout the year.

Charlton Mackrell

The parish of Charlton Mackrell includes four small villages – Charlton Adam, Charlton Mackrell, Lytes Cary and Cary Fitzpaine.

It may number under 1,000 souls but the parish has had its place on the map since the earliest times of recorded history. The Romans built the main road, the Fosse Way, and they quarried the blue lias stone to build Lindinnis (now known as Ilchester). Field names go back to Saxon days and the lay-out of the manors can still be traced by the lay-out of the villages.

You can visit a typical Somerset manor house, thanks to its last owner Sir Walter Jenner and the National Trust, at Lytes Cary. Its chapel dates from 1343 and the Lyte family lived there for 500 years (13th–18th centuries). In 1578 Henry Lyte published the most famous horticultural book of his day, the *Niewe Herball*.

For long centuries the villages were part of church-owned lands. Then the Dissolution of the Monasteries in the 1530s caused a tremendous upset. The Cary Fitzpaine estate was sold to Henry Courtenay, Earl of Devon, who promptly got into trouble with Henry VIII and was executed for treason. Later Queen Elizabeth I made a present of land in the same area to her favourite Sir Francis Walsingham.

Henry Adams was married at Charlton Mackrell church in 1609 and in 1638 when Henry was 55 years of age he crossed the Atlantic with his family in a small boat. Henry Adams' great grandson was John Adams who steered through the United States Congress the Declaration of Independence in 1776. He became the 2nd President of the USA and his son John Quincy Adams was the 6th President. There are still some descendants of the Adams family living in Charlton Adam.

The population has risen and fallen according to the economics of the times. At one time there was a medieval village in the area now known as West Charlton. The advent of the motor car and modern farming methods have had their effect. Once there was a railway station, now the trains pass by. Once there were 14 shops, now down to one post office/store in Charlton Adam and one shop in Charlton Mackrell. But still there is the school and the population is growing again.

Charlton Musgrove ✖

Charlton Musgrove is in many respects a surprising place. It is one of those villages which appears to the casual passerby to have no beginning and no end, with no perceptible main street. There is a small post office/general store which has operated for over 60 years, but even this takes some finding by the uninitiated! The old village school stands in the same street, but closed some 25 years ago, when pupils were provided with bicycles to transport themselves to nearby Wincanton.

In Anglo-Saxon times, the village was known as Cerletone. By the end of the 12th century it was in the possession of the Norman family of Mucegros, and when John de Mucegros (died 1275) took up residence here, the family name was added to Cereltone to distinguish it from similar place-names in the region.

It is, and always has been, a predominantly agricultural community and evidence still remains of the old medieval village near Lower Church Farm. The farmhouse itself was erected in 1738 on the site of a much earlier building, and remains suggest the past existence of a 3-acre orchard of cider apples. A dairy still stands, where cheese was made and hauled upstairs through a hole in the ceiling, to stand on shelves, the slats of which can be seen today.

Clearly central to the community for many centuries, the parish church of St Stephen dates from the 13th century, but has been much altered and enlarged. Between 1617 and 1914 the incumbents were all members of the heir family who also held the advowson of the living until 1976. They were amongst the last of the so-called 'squarsons' or squire-parsons, and their prominence underlines the clear inter-reliance of church and land-owner.

Perhaps the building of greatest historical interest in Charlton Mus-grove is Stavordale Priory, the name of which is thought to be derived from the fact that it lies in a 'Dell of the Stour'. It was founded by Lord Richard Lovel some time in the first half of the 13th century. Allowed to decay for many years, the priory was rescued from disaster earlier this century when a new owner undertook to restore and preserve what remained of the original. The work has been continued by the present owners, who have spared no expense in preserving the priory's very fine architectural features.

The Lovels were the family who achieved notoriety thanks to the 19th century songwriter T. H. Bayley's somewhat macabre song *The Mistletoe*

Bough. It tells the story of the Lovel bride who, playing hide and seek on her wedding night, hid in an old chest, the lid of which accidentally locked shut. Many years later her skeleton was found in the chest, still clothed in her wedding gown.

Cheddar 🌿

The name of the village is thought to come from two Celtic words 'ced' meaning 'height' and 'dwr' meaning 'water', which probably refers to the cliffs and the river. The cliffs, of course, are well-known, and the river, which flows through the caves and then runs peacefully down beside the road to the gorge, once provided the power for several mills and work for many villagers.

The lives of Cheddar folk were changed considerably after the opening of the caves, the first of which was discovered accidentally in 1837. Further caves were discovered in 1877 and recently, during excavation, evidence has been found which shows that early Cheddar cave-men were cannibals. With each new discovery more and more tourists flock to the village. Before the caves opened, Cheddar had been a quiet little village consisting of four or five irregular streets. When the broad-gauge railway line to Bristol opened in 1869 tourists arrived at the brand new Brunel-designed Railway Station. Soon others came on the newly invented bicycles. The Cliff Hotel had been the head-quarters of the Cyclists' Touring Club since its formation. One can imagine Victorian and Edwardian lady cyclists in their long and unsuitable skirts struggling into Cheddar. They were no doubt glad to sit down in the Cliff Hotel tea-garden and rest before the great adventure of seeing the caves and then pedalling off again.

The fame of Cheddar grew and soon more shops and cafes opened to cater for the needs of the tourists. Almost everything imaginable had 'A Present from Cheddar' stamped on it. Today thousands of people from all over the world visit the Gorge and Caves and sample our delicious strawberries and cream. Strawberries grow well on the warm slopes of the Mendips. Whilst the lives of many Cheddar people are centred on the tourist industry in one way or another, the Gorge and Caves are not the only parts of the village which are of interest.

Cheddar has always been a busy place. Weekly markets were held near the 15th century Market Cross up to the middle of the 18th century and it was here that the famous Cheddar cheeses, which have been made in the district for 700 years, were sold. Now the noise and bustle of the market is gone and the Market Cross provides a shady resting place for the old and young of the village.

The village had reason to celebrate on August 29th 1889 for it was the centenary of the opening of Cheddar's first Sunday School and School in the Hannah More Cottage in Lower North Street (now the meeting place of the Evergreen Club). The experiment was so successful that other schools sprang up in villages around Cheddar and education in the Cheddar Valley was on its way. Today it has reached a very high standard.

It was purely by chance that the place chosen for this celebration was a field called Yeodens (pronounced Yawdens). Little did the villagers know, as they sat down to tea in a large tent, that they were on the site of the future Kings of Wessex School, or that under their feet were the remains of King Alfred's Palace. The palace was discovered during the building of the school and stones marking the site can be seen in the grounds of the school. This was where Assemblies, or Witans, were held between AD 901 and 968.

Local industry is changing. The strawberry crop is still important and the season well patronised, but other industries are making their mark and a small industrial park is growing in and around the old railway station.

The village today is a mixture of old and new. There are still some picturesque parts of old Cheddar and there are also many new housing estates. It is no longer a village where everyone knows everyone else. Indeed some people do not even know all the roads in the village! It is still, though, an interesting and pleasant place in which to live.

Cheddon Fitzpaine ✣

Cheddon Fitzpaine is situated 2½ miles north of Taunton, at the foot of the Quantocks. At the time of the Domesday survey, Opcedre and Cedre (Upper Cheddon and Cheddon) were amongst the estates held by Robert Arundel.

The Warre family came to Hestercombe in King Charles I's reign and several Warres have been Rectors. Hestercombe House and estate was purchased by Viscount Portman and then sold to the Crown Estate Commissioners in 1945. In subsequent years there have been many changes. Hestercombe House is now the property of Somerset County

Council, and is used as the headquarters of the Somerset Fire Brigade. The restored gardens, designed by Sir Edwin Lutyens and Gertrude Jekyll, are opened to the public.

The church, whose pulpit and font are worth noting, has been in need of constant restoration to the medieval tower and surrounding parapet. Both old and new rectories have been sold, with the rectorial living now in plurality with Kingston St Mary and Broomfield. Services are held once weekly.

Some of the southern part of the village has gone from sweet meadowland to industrial sites and a rubbish disposal tip.

In the early 1950s a farm was developed for housing, and a rural electorate of 240 became 1640, with subsequent repercussions! In 1987, this housing area was taken into Taunton Wards. Now, although the village was made a listed village and in a Green Wedge, there are planning proposals to build 850 houses and new roads etc to attract commuters from Bristol and Exeter.

There is, however, one farming family – Musgrave by name – who have been farming in the village for nearly 300 years. The farms are mostly dairy, corn growing, sheep and beef. There is one nursery garden. Farm door-sales are lively near to the housing estates. Another trend is for livery stables attached to farms. This can cause some road usage difficulties!

There is a comprehensive school at Ladymead and the junior school for Kings College at Pyrland. Our C. of E. V.C. Primary school has about 80–90 pupils mainly from the Taunton estates catchment area.

There is no pub or a village shop, but there is a post office, which is a great benefit to the elderly in particular. There is also a shoeing smith and blacksmith – a metalworker. Village life is mainly around the Memorial Hall, maintained by devoted volunteers.

Chewton Mendip

The Norman church of St Mary Magdalen has one of the most beautiful 'Somerset Towers', 126 feet high, for which the County is famous. Inside is a 'frid stool', a very rare sanctuary seat, a lectern made especially for the 1611 Bible upon it, and a chalice and paten dated 1511. Chewton is the home of the Waldegrave family. They now run a prospering cheese manufactury in the village.

Chilcompton 🍃

Although, like its famous neighbours Bath and Wells, Chilcompton is growing day by day to meet the needs of modern families, it still retains what most newcomers seek, its village atmosphere and friendliness.

It was known in the Domesday Book as Contone, and its present name is said to be derived from the old words 'ceald' – cold, 'combe' – valley, and 'ton' – village. It is certainly true that the winds in the highest point can be particularly cutting, but it is always pleasant to walk by the little stream with daffodils on its banks, and to feed the ducks which cross the road in their own good time, regardless of the traffic.

There are several old houses in the village, one of which, Gainsborough House, belonged to the painter Gainsborough when Bath was in its heyday, with Nash, Ralph Allen and John Palmer furnishing it.

Today jet aircraft fly overhead but when Gainsborough lived in the village, Royal Mail coaches *then* known as the 'flying machines' ran through Chilcompton. In more modern times the *Pines Express* was silhouetted against the sky-line under great clouds of steam, as it laboured its way to Bournemouth. Now we pick blackberries and walk over the track, hardly realising that it ever existed. And the spirit of Chilcompton is still vigorous. The village hall which is light and spacious, was built with money raised by the villagers, and is the centre of village life. The villagers also painted a mural over the stage, which shows life as it is in Chilcompton today.

Chilthorne Domer 🍃

Chilthorne Domer was a manor of the Earl of Morton at the time of the Norman Conquest. It derived its name from Sir John de Domer, who married a local girl, a daughter of the Vagg family.

The 14th century church, St Mary's, is built in the local Hamstone, which was brought by cart from the quarry, six miles away. St Mary's has a bell cote instead of a tower. On the bell tower there is a crucifix on which is carved the figure of our Lord. The interior is very beautiful, with some very fine carving and Jacobean seating throughout. Within the altar rails on the north side, under an arch is the recumbent figure of a knight clad in a coat of mail, thought to be Sir William de Domer (father of Sir John de Domer).

44

There are several beautiful farmhouses, also a small manor house where there is an outside communal loo, which was built around 1720. The six seats are arranged round three sides of the building, which is only 10 feet by 10 feet. The loo sits over a stream which no doubt distributed the effluent – in its day!

Chilthorne has a flourishing community, with a village school, hall, recreational club and playing field. The inhabitants of about 400 are well catered for, with a post office/village shop and two public houses, with a very picturesque main street through the village.

Several events are held during the year, the main attractions being the Village Fete and Garden Show, which are organised in the old traditional way.

The Garden Show has been held for the past 5 years and is strictly restricted to villagers. Feelings run high when the day comes and one must confess the entry closing time is never stuck to, because of older competitors having a crafty peep at their rivals' produce, before popping in an apologetic late entry.

Wine making has a class at the show, but was nearly placed on probation when one year, the judges got carried away and demolished half a bottle of someone's prize wine, only to leave an apologetic note to say 'an agreement could not be reached to its taste'. That's village life isn't it?

Chilton Polden 🐾

About midway along the ridge of the Polden Hills stands Chilton Priory, alongside the A39 (originally a Roman road), overlooking the village of Chilton Polden and the Somerset Levels to the north and south.

The tower and chapel were completed in 1836 when a builder, George Dowden, who lived in Goose Lane, was engaged to carry out the construction for William Stradling, a local historian and collector. His ancestral home was a castle in South Wales which could be seen from the tower on a clear day. His home in the village was the Tower House, a large Georgian property which also boasts a tower in the grounds, visible from the other two. The dwelling-house was added about 1900.

Until quite recently, Chilton Polden observed a Shrove Tuesday custom. The church bells were rung at noon, whereupon the housewives would rush outside banging pans and shouting 'Pan, Pan'. The children were given a half-day holiday, and went through the streets singing a song:

> Shrove Tuesday, Shrove Tuesday,
> When Jack went to plough,
> His mother made pancakes
> She did not know how.
> She tossed them, she turned them,
> She made them so black,
> She put on so much pepper
> She poisoned poor Jack. Hooray.

The rhyme has not been heard for many years, but for 70 years baker Oliver Coombes, and then his successor, made a pancake for every child in the parish.

The village, like most rural communities, remained almost self-sufficient until the First World War, and many small businesses continued until 1939, although by that time a daily omnibus had replaced the carrier's cart to Bridgwater.

Now the majority of residents travel to work, usually by car, to the neighbouring towns of Bridgwater and Street. Primary schoolchildren attend school in Catcott, and older children are bussed to Street. However, there still remains the church, a post office, a general store, a garage, a pub, farms, builders and several small thriving businesses.

Chiselborough

Chiselborough lies in a sheltered valley surrounded by five hills, Gawlers, Pease, Brympton, Pen and Balham. In Saxon times it was called Ceolsebergon (gravel hill). In 1987 there were about 250 residents, including a fair proportion of young people with varying occupations in the surrounding district. It is no longer a farming community.

Much of the village was owned by the Lords of the Manor of Ilchester until 1914, when it was sold off in lots by auction. The common was also owned by them, but is now in the possession of the parish. Fairplace, as it is called, is inhabited by a variety of wildlife and a number of rare wild flowers, the smaller ones being in danger unless it continues to be grazed. From the common one gets a scenic view of the village and the countryside beyond. It is sheltered from the north by Gawlers Hill (425 feet).

Fairplace is aptly named, being the site of an October fair which was founded in 1257 and continued until 1894. Legend has it that the men of Hinton St George were, on one occasion, making merry at the fair. When they did not return home, their wives made 'punkies', that is candle lanterns made from hollowed-out mangolds with strange faces cut in them, and came looking for them. The men were terrified, and fled home, much to their wives' amusement. A Punky night is still held in Chiselborough at the end of October, when children make mangold lanterns and prizes are awarded for the best ones.

The parish church is dedicated to St Peter and St Paul, and has a low central tower between the nave and the chancel. An octagonal spire was added in the 13th century, one of the few in Somerset. Many additions have been made over the centuries, and the Victorian nave ceiling was replaced in 1980–81. There are five bells, the oldest 14th century, and they are regularly rung, the ringers standing on the floor between nave and chancel. The Langdon family has been associated with the parish church since 1770, as parish clerks and as organists.

The village hall, The Ilchester Hall, named after the Manor, was built in 1870, and was formerly the village school. Strapp farmhouse, built in

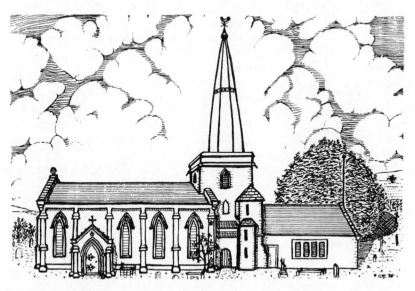

The church of St Peter & St Paul, Chiselborough

47

1576, is of interest with its mullioned windows and cambered door-head, although it is no longer a farmhouse.

The mill pond at Manor Farm originally fed a waterwheel which was constructed in 1861 to provide power to the farm buildings for rolling cattle feed, chaff cutting, sheep shearing etc. It was fed by springs rising at the top of the village at Brooksway. Unfortunately the wheel and most of the shafting was removed for scrap during the war and the pond silted up. Since 1986, the owners, the Holloways, have re-instated the pond, with the help of a grant from the Farm Wildlife Advisory Group. Trees have been planted and the pond has been restocked with fish, namely carp.

Clapton 🌿

Clapton is a small village of around 60 houses, situated up on the edge of the Mendips, between Midsomer Norton and Ston Easton. The name is derived from the Old English words 'clop', a hill, and 'tun', an enclosure or settlement. The name seems an apt one. From this modest altitude, there are fine views over the surrounding countryside. We also have to expect slightly later growing seasons with more winds and weather.

Two inhabitants, Len and Mary Gulliford, are well-known in the county for their bees and honey. You will find them at the Bath and West and other local agricultural shows.

In recent years, the major preoccupation of many of the villagers has been the building of a new village hall. In the building of the hall, a small stone was found inscribed with a rough Star of David, plus the figures 6 6 6. We have long puzzled about who put the stone there and why. The Book of Revelation tells us that 6 6 6 was a reference to the Beast, alias apparently King Herod. There is also mention of the Star of David. We wonder whether the stone is associated with black magic or perhaps a warning. We have never arrived at any satisfactory explanation and would welcome any further suggestions.

Buildings of any town or village form an intriguing historical record. Those of Clapton are no exception. The village must have been very small, as there is no Church of England church. However, the rise of Methodism in the 18th century found fertile ground here. It is the site of an early Zion chapel, while the present chapel is a fine example of Victorian Byzantine. The earliest houses are former farms and cottages from the Tudor and Stuart age. They are built in the local limestone. The

48

style of the farmhouses makes one conclude that farming was prosperous then.

There is evidence of great agricultural change taking place in the late 18th century with the enclosure of open land with walls of Mendip stone. The 19th century saw the rise of coal mining and the building of two small terraces of miners' cottages. One of the farmhouses became a public house which with much alteration continues to flourish today. During the early part of the present century, a small quarry developed within the village. Today, it is a cement block works. After the Second World War, eight council houses and more latterly a handful of private bungalows and houses were erected.

Today, the farms are fewer. Mining has gone. Now, the inhabitants are mainly employed in the surrounding towns.

Combe Florey 🦋

The first mention of Combe Florey was in 1100 when Baldwin de Cume, or Combe, lived at the manor house. Baldwin probably took his name from Combe, meaning a valley. Baldwin de Cume was succeeded, about the time of King Stephen (1135–1154), by Hugh de Fleuri, or Flory, probably of Norman origin, and by his son Randolph, who gave his name to the village.

Combe Florey is a tiny village with a population of some 150, situated at the foot of the Quantocks, surrounded by pear orchards and as pretty as its name suggests. It is small wonder then that it has, in its time, housed a number of eminent men.

In the early 19th century the celebrated cleric and wit, Sidney Smith, canon of St Paul's Cathedral, lived in the Old Rectory where he 'grew old merrily', and wonderful stories are told of his sense of fun. It seems he would try to deceive his London friends by tying oranges on to his laurel bushes and putting antlers on to his donkeys so that when he took his guests into his garden after dinner, as the light was fading, they would be impressed by his orangery and his herd of deer!

In the Old Manor House, which has a beautiful oratory window over the porch, and some fine plasterwork, the Rattigan family lived. They left in 1924 and Terence Rattigan later became well-known as a popular playwright. Evelyn Waugh brought his wife and large family to Combe Florey in 1957, and his son Auberon, a writer like his father, now lives here. Combe Florey House stands high above the village and it is reached by way of an impressive and most attractive gatehouse built in 1593.

The church, dating from the 13th century, has many interesting features. The stone effigies lying in the north aisle are thought to be of Sir John de Meriet and his two wives, Mary who died aged 18 and his second wife Elizabeth, who died in 1344. There is also a little heart shrine in the wall belonging to a nun of Cannington Priory who lived in the second half of the 13th century. The carved pews are very fine and there are two attractive brasses.

Combwich 🐚

A community grew up here at the point at which the tidal estuary of the river Parrett could be forded at low tide and crossed by ferry at high tide, linking North Somerset with the Exmoor district and North Devon. The first settlement was at Otterhampton a mile and a half to the north-west of Combwich where enemy ships could be more easily observed from an elevated position.

Combwich, pronounced 'Cummidge', derives its name from the legend surrounding Dame Withycombe, a witch by repute, who lived in a cottage near the village, from whom it became known as 'Combe of the Witch'.

One alarming aspect of the close proximity of the river has been the incidence of flooding up to recent times. This threat has now been alleviated by the construction of a tidal defence wall completed in 1987, enclosing the common and totally altering the face of the riverfront. A spectacular bore effect occurs here in about March.

Since Roman times Combwich has been an important port used by shipping from Europe and the Americas. Many of the buildings of the village date from Victorian times when the Combwich and District Farmers Association among others ran a busy fleet. The thriving sea captains built residences and warehouses around the Pill where the ships were anchored, one of the most imposing being the Tower House, with its lookout where the Leigh family could observe the coming and going of their coal vessels. The port later silted up but has been reconstructed this century with the coming of Hinkley Point Nuclear Power Station.

In the 18th century a thriving brickyard grew up utilising the thick deposits of clay laid down in flood tides. Winters could be difficult for the brickyard workers as a hard frost often cracked the tiles meaning loss of work for many weeks in a severe season. Today it is the site of a modern housing estate with the 40 foot fishing ponds left after the clay extraction forming a pleasant outlook for the residents.

Until the turn of the century it was customary to hold a Wassail Ceremony in January in the prolific parish orchards. Guns were fired into the trees and bread soaked in cider placed in the fork of a tree for the robins to bring good luck and a fruitful season. The Combwich version of the Somerset Wassail Song was sung and large measures of cider consumed in traditional two-handled cups.

Compton Dundon 🐚

> Compton Dundon is a pretty place
> It lies down in a valley.
> Dundon has the ring of bells
> And Compton the skittle alley.

Compton Dundon is a village situated between Street and Somerton, surrounded by hills. Compton is at the foot of Butleigh Woods, while Dundon half-circles a cone-shaped hill with an ancient camp at its summit named Dundon Beacon and is 300 feet high. The camp was an Iron Age settlement and there is evidence of Roman occupation.

The village school was built in 1873. At the end of the first year there were 33 pupils and now there are 56. In bygone days absenteeism at the school was a problem, caused chiefly by the demands of the village community. In April 1886 it was recorded, 'Half of the children are absent this week, picking primroses for a man who comes here twice a week, buys them and sends them to London'. Despite this, there are still banks full of primroses to be seen in the village every year.

The village hall, originally a chapel, was given to the village by Mr Edmund Page of Ivythorne Manor in 1937 and it is in use most nights. There is a post office with general stores and one pub, The Castlebrook Inn, which serve the village well. The Castlebrook is the home alley to six skittle teams.

Dairy farming is the main industry but with the milk quotas, many more farmers are keeping sheep or growing more cereals. The thatchers, whose family has been in the village for 200 years, and whose work is visible around the village, are kept very busy but they still find time to appear on television quite often. The village boasts quite a few smaller industries, from engineering to snail farming.

The 13th century church stands at the top of Dundon. Inside the church there is a delightful Jacobean pulpit. It is reached through an old roodloft doorway and has back panels, side balustrade, a carved cornice and a seat inside. The branches of the churchyard yew shade a space about as big as the church itself and is reputed to be over 1,000 years old. Its hollow trunk has room for several people to stand inside, but beware, if you lose your child in the churchyard, the gap is closing!

Combe St Nicholas

Combe St Nicholas has barrows from the Bronze Age, and a small museum in the church which contains a shell, buried when the area was under the sea, Roman horseshoes, and part of a screen dated 1480. A Roman pavement was found at Higher Wadeford, but has been destroyed by the weather. The home of the Bonner family was a Tudor farmhouse named 'Weston', still with fine plaster ceilings, and a stout bar to draw across the old door.

Corfe

Corfe is a small, pretty village on the northern slopes of the Blackdown Hills, four miles south of Taunton. The name is said to have derived from an ancient word meaning 'gap' or 'pass' and this is borne out by the cleft in the hillside which takes the Honiton road over the Blackdowns from the village. Although it is not mentioned in the Domesday Book the village has existed since Norman times. It is known that a priory farm was established in medieval times and after the Dissolution of the Monasteries the land was sold to a lawyer, Humphrey Colles, who built a tremendous house, known as Barton, of which only the large servants' wing remains and this has been converted into flats. The property was the residence of the Newton family for many years until the beginning of this century, known by then as Barton Grange, and the family still owns much of the surrounding farmland.

Calamine and limestone were quarried on the hills around the village and there were numerous lime kilns for burning the lime for agricultural use. The site of the main calamine workings was transformed into a golf course in the 19th century where it still flourishes. The ancient woodlands which provided the fuel for the kilns remain and provide a magnificent backcloth to the village.

Corfe has a population of a little over 200, with houses dating from the 16th century to the present day, stretching along the sides of the B3170, and with the hamlets of Adcombe and Heale. The village shop and post office is in the centre of the village and provides much needed services to the village and the surrounding area.

The church of St Nicholas shares its vicar with Pitminster. A Norman church, it was rebuilt in the 19th century. It is very well maintained in an excellent condition, and supported by devoted and hard-working parishioners. Opposite the church by the approach road to Barton Grange stands the village hall, adjacent to the Queen's Acre, a recreation ground given to the village by the Newton family, local landowners, to commemorate Queen Victoria's Diamond Jubilee.

By the church stand Church Cottages, a row of old thatched houses which, with the grass lawn in front of them, provide a very pleasant prospect, enhanced by mature trees throughout the village. The general appearance of the village has helped it to win the Best Kept Small Village competition in Somerset on a number of occasions.

There are now only three working farms left in Corfe, one at either end of the village, and one at Heale; the baker, the smithy, and the butcher and slaughter house have long since gone, and most of the employment has moved to Taunton to which residents commute. Many of the villagers are retired although there are several young families whose children go to the primary schools at Pitminster or Thurlbear, neighbouring villages, or to senior schools in Taunton. Corfe school closed some years ago and is now a private house.

Cossington 🎝

Cossington is a very welcoming village situated on the west side of the Poldens. The church, school and village hall are the three main focuses in the village, together with the post office and general store and butcher's shop.

A thatched cottage standing on the corner of the A39 leading down into Cossington was once a lodge for the keeper of the estate. It was restored in 1900 but with history dating back to 1254 when the Brett family ruled the manor.

Today the village has many activities and everyone is well catered for, from playgroup to Friends and Neighbours club. Cossington is a very happy village.

The big tree which was a famous landmark in the village is now just a stump surrounded by concrete and planted with heathers in the top. This was one of the disasters of the Dutch Elm disease. It was said that John Wesley preached under it.

Coxley 🐝

Coxley lies on the A39 Wells to Glastonbury Road and is said to be the last village on the Mendips and the first on the Somerset Levels, consequently we have the best of both world. The name is pronounced Cokesly and not Coxley as in 'box'.

The original village was probably to the south-east of the present main road, as old maps show many more dwellings at Upper Coxley and a road which no longer exists. There are still a number of old cottages in this area including one which was the old post office.

The little Victorian church is one of the few buildings that anyone passing through the village today would notice as it stands on high ground, but there are one or two interesting older buildings. The Pound Inn is 200 years old and its name draws attention to the fact that nearby there was once a pound where stray animals were put.

The names of some of the properties and fields give one clues to the past way of life here. For instance, near Littlewell Farm was a well where the villagers who had no wells of their own would draw their drinking water before the advent of a piped water supply. And along Mill Lane is, as you would expect, an old mill house which is thought to have been built on the site of an earlier building, probably a barn, in the early 1700s. The mill was built on to the house, both being constructed of local stone. The house is still very attractive and well maintained with the original elegant fan-light over the front door. The mill stream used to run under the house and one can see where the wheel would have been during the working life of the mill. It is said that the lavatories were positioned over the water-wheel, very practical!

The cider apple orchards which once abounded here have now largely disappeared but the area is still mainly agricultural. Most of the farms are dairy farms and there are some sheep and pigs. There is also one farmer who breeds and shows heavy horses.

The village is fortunate in having a post office/general store as well as a village hall, a garage, a vineyard and a school which is still open – long may it be so!

Cranmore

West Cranmore lies clustered around St Bartholomew's church. The village was built up by the Strode family, wool merchants, at the same time that they built their country seat, Southill House. Before this there was, no doubt, a late medieval village here since the church dates from the 16th century. However there remains very little evidence of this earlier period save the church and an old churchyard cross.

Southill House, the seat of the Strode family, was built in the mid 1700s. The family lived there until the later 1800s when the house was bought by the Spencer family, brewers of Oakhill, together with the Strode estate. Southill House has been altered through the ages but remains much the same as it was when first built.

The old parish of East Cranmore was inhabited earlier than West Cranmore, having a Saxon church which, in the early 1800s, was extensively renovated in the Gothic style. The Paget family, who lived at Cranmore Hall and were Lords of the Manor of East Cranmore from the 1790s until the 1950s, renovated the Hall and the church and built an ornate tower on the hill above their estate.

Cranmore Tower, which stands on the hill above East Cranmore, was built by John Moore Paget to designs drawn up by Thomas Wyatt. The work commenced in 1863, with the marking out of the site, and was completed in September 1865.

During the Second World War the Tower was used by both the Home Guard and the Armed Forces and was therefore not open to the curious. It had, in fact, never been open to the public as such, the members of the Paget family using it for their own private uses. Members of the Paget estate servants' families were sometimes allowed access and it was the site of prearranged Sunday School picnics and other estate jollifications. Both East and West Cranmore families grew used to attending these functions at the invitation of the Paget family.

Access to the Tower is through well ridden and walked bridle-paths. There is no public access by motor vehicle and this benefits the local community since it remains one of the few places locally to be safe for riders, young and old, and free from traffic. There is also a good network of public footpaths on 'Tower' hill for those seeking a walk, with a good choice of views.

Croscombe

In Saxon times, as early as AD 705, Croscombe was 'on the map', appearing as Correges cumb, but by 1309 it had become known as Corscombe. Its old houses mostly lie cheek by jowl, half-way along the delightful valley which slopes down from Shepton Mallet to Wells, following the stream labelled river Sheppey by the Ordnance Survey. Would that the map-makers had observed the local name of Doulting Water, since the stream rises from the holy well of St Aldhelm just below the church at Doulting.

It is to the grassy hillsides of the valley and the clear swiftly flowing stream, that Croscombe owes its development and time of prosperity in the 16th and 17th centuries when the population was in the region of 600. On the hillsides the sheep grazed and produced wool, while the stream provided water to wash the woollen cloth woven by the industrious cottagers. Lower Mill was probably at first a fulling mill where the cloth was doused with fullers earth and water, then pounded to remove the grease and dirt. The area known as Rack Close (where the village hall now stands) was where the finished cloth was stretched on tenter frames to dry. Two 17th century buildings, Cliff View House (once a weaver's cottage) and Ashley House (originally an early weaving 'factory') remind us of the industry.

The church contains many reminders of the village's wealthy past and is well worth a visit. Its chief glory is its splendid Jacobean woodwork.

Greatly valued today is the flourishing village school of about 70 pupils. Its roots go back to a Dame School of the early 1800s on the same site, and the imposing structure which we see today was built in 1870.

Markets were a fillip to trade and a measure of a developing community. In the 13th century Edward I granted Croscombe a weekly market (Tuesdays) and an annual fair on Lady Day, and later monarchs ratified this. A wide range of goods from food and livestock to cloth and clothing were traded, centred around the steps of the Market Cross at the bottom of Church Street, but it seems to have lapsed by the late 18th century. Through the energy of a small group of local women, it was restarted in

The village of Croscombe

1967 and continues as a useful and enjoyable village occasion, though no longer exposed to the elements around the Cross!

The Market Cross, still a conspicuous landmark on the main road, was raised in the 14th century with its 3 steps and 8 foot shaft. But since the top was mutilated, presumably after the Puritan inspired Parliamentary order, it has been topped by a faceted ball. In the 1870s the local Waywardens, deciding that the Cross impeded the highway, started to remove it and broke the shaft. The incensed villagers attacked and battle ensued, ending in the retreat of the Wardens, while 30 men of the village made a bivouac for the night around an open fire. Thus was the cross saved! Not so the stocks which stood alongside at one time, but have now disappeared.

With the Industrial Revolution, the wool-weaving (and by that time, also silk and linen) tended to move from the village cottage to factories in towns, and by the 19th century, times were bad in Croscombe. Prosperity faded and today we have two shops (one a post office), two pubs, numerous small businesses and a friendly, lively community.

Crowcombe 🪶

Crowcombe, nestling on the south-western slopes of the Quantocks retains today all the essentials of a small rural community where little has really changed for 400 years. The parish is made up of the main village together with an area known as Crowcombe Heathfield (where Crowcombe Station and Youth Hostel are situated) to the south, and scattered farms covering a lozenge-shaped area of some 3,271 acres.

The village still has a squire who owns a number of the cottages and a good deal of the surrounding land and farms. Crowcombe Court which was built around 1739 and has been described as one of the finest houses of its date south of Bath, is no longer his manor house but is now an old people's home. Close to the centre of the village are those essentials for good village life: the church, pub and school.

Opposite the church (which is worth a visit to see the carved bench-ends dating from 1534) is the Church House. This building was known

Crowcombe Court, built in 1739

58

to have been in existence by 1520 and was built as a place for the village to disport itself and hold 'church ales' and other similar events and still functions as the village hall today. It has a magnificent timber roof and is open to the public on weekday afternoons in the summer. The school dates from 1872 (though the Carew family provided schooling for the village before that) and had an average attendance in 1889 of 55 pupils. Today it is a Church primary school drawing children up to the age of 9 from a number of local villages and attendances are still between 40–50.

There has been an innkeeper in the parish since 1620 and the present pub still retains the traditional stone flagged floors and wooden tables and benches, which would have been familiar to anyone visiting the doctor's surgery held in the public bar until the early 1950s and well remembered by some of the village's older residents.

Crowcombe once had a charter to hold a weekly market and the old medieval Butter Cross still stands opposite the pub to prove it. Today the village is lucky still to retain its post office and to have a village shop, lucky too to have a mixed community which includes a balance of children, working adults and pensioners.

Curry Mallet & Beercrocombe

Curry Mallet, a small unspoilt village of some 300 inhabitants, is almost entirely owned by His Royal Highness Prince Charles, as one of his Duchy of Cornwall estates. The Prince is a frequent visitor to the tenant farms of the village.

The village boasts a lovely old manor house, parts of which date back to before the Norman Conquest.

Curry Mallet also has a very fine 15th century church. Every year in early January the medieval service of Blessing the Plough is still held. The farmers bring the seed corn to be blessed and the farm workers and various tradesmen bring their tools of trade and process to the altar, followed by the plough which is carried in. The ancient plough is kept permanently in the church.

Although two separate villages, differing in many ways, Curry Mallet and Beercrocombe were once linked by the old Chard to Taunton canal. This was opened in 1842 and closed only 25 years later, but parts of the old canal can still be seen today. Between Curry Mallet and Beercrocombe there stands a house with the name of Star Farm. It stands next to the canal and when this was being constructed, the farmhouse was turned into a pub and renamed 'Star Inn', to serve the gangs of workmen on the canal and later the canal boatmen.

Nearby, the canal ran into Crimson Hill tunnel which is 1,800 yards long, one of the longest in Britain.

Tub boats rather than long boats ran this canal and in the roof of the tunnel were shackles to help the boatmen haul their boats through, they did not 'leg' them as long boatmen did.

At the far end of Beercrocombe lies Keyses Farm. Many years ago this farm was well known for its May Fairs, which were held on the first three Sundays in May. They started early in the morning, but finished at 6p.m. to allow the farmers and their workers to do the evening milking. All the local people came to enjoy themselves on the swing-boats, merry-go-rounds etc. All of the young lads and lassies took part in the annual rounders matches. Each village had its own team and there was fierce competition. They were kept refreshed by plenty of pies and bread and cheese, washed down with gallons of local cider. After tea, they all went to see the healing spring, most folk swore it had magic powers. Some would drink from it to cure their ills, some would wash in it, hoping it would clear their spots, others would pour the water over their feet to cure gout.

Curry Rivel 🌿

The village of Curry Rivel sprawls along a three mile stretch of the A378 as it pursues its busy way along the gently rising ridge to Taunton. The few remaining empty spaces provide excellent views down the steep northern slopes to Sedgemoor and the gentle southern slopes to the Ile Valley. In exceptionally wet weather the valley fields, lying underwater for much of the winter, provide a resting place for a plentiful supply of wild-fowl for the enthusiastic bird watcher.

The Revel family, Lords of the Manor in the 12th century undoubtedly gave Curry Rivel the second part of its name, but the first part, with many suggested and some quite plausible origins, remains an unsolved mystery.

The magnificent church of St Andrew with its famous Jennings Memorial (two brothers in Trooper uniforms with their wives and children kneeling around them, while tucked up into two tiny stone beds are twins and triplets who died in infancy) stands on The Green about 200 yards to

Curry Rivel village green

the north of the main road. The brothers, Robert and Marmaduke Jennings who died in 1625 and 1630, lived and farmed at Burton Farm.

In the churchyard stands the Old Schoolroom, a listed building, where children's clubs and groups meet on a regular basis.

In the shadow of the church lies the village hall, built by and presented to the village in 1908 by Robert Sewers, a local businessman who having made a fortune as a jeweller in London wished to make a contribution to the home of his youth. The hall is in constant use by local organisations.

Unique among the revellers on Old Christmas Night, the wassailers of Curry Rivel enjoy the traditional burning of the Ashen Faggot. After singing the wassail song around the village, calling enroute at various houses for refreshment, the wassailers return to the King William IV Inn to burn the faggot. It is bound with thongs, and as each thong bursts the assembled company call for 'free drinks on the house'. The Inn is crowded!

Visible for miles around stands 'The Monument', erected by the First

Earl of Chatham, as a token of gratitude to William Pynsent, who had bequeathed to him his house and manor. The Pitt family came to live in Curry Rivel in 1765 and William, the Earl's second son, became Britain's youngest Prime Minister.

The village is well endowed with shops and with two inns and a restaurant in the restored Old Forge (the cellar with its massive vaulted ceiling is a must for anyone interested in ancient buildings).

Cutcombe & Wheddon Cross 🦩

Who knows about Udicombe? Very few of us. It is under this strange sounding name, that one finds it mentioned in the Domesday Book. Documents of a later date call the hilltop village Codecombe. The exact change to Cutcombe is not known. Nestling near the foot of the hill called Dunkery Beacon (at 1770 feet the highest hill in the West), it commands from the stone cross standing near the church porch a magnificent view down to the coast and on clear days right across the Bristol Channel.

Back in the 18th century, Mr Richard Ellsworth founded the parochial school, to educate over 100 poor children to be 'able to read, write and say their catechism'. Neighbouring Timberscombe equally benefited from Mr Ellsworth's gift. The buildings of the boys' and girls' schools still stand and are now comfortable private homes. In 1875 a schoolhouse for the headmaster's use and a school for 200 children were built. Both of these still display their original facade, whilst inside they provide modern facilities for a diminished, yet steadily increasing number of first school pupils. Children come from neighbouring and even more distant parishes, owing to the excellent education provided for them.

The village hall, known as Moorland Hall, together with the playing fields, children's play area and the recently erected sports pavilion, provides physical, social, educational, cultural and musical facilities not just for the parishioners, but for various other groups for diverse functions.

The phrase 'where time runs slowly' (and buses hardly run at all) fits Cutcombe village perfectly. Tranquillity is the true characteristic of this village 'behind God's back'. Yet the villagers are as busy as bees in a hive. Lambing, sheering, dipping, hedging, haymaking, milking; housing and feeding visitors from Easter till late autumn; jumble sales, carol singing, bell-ringing, keep-fit classes, painting classes, whist drives, discos fill time of work and leisure.

Early in the 19th century, 450 souls lived in Cutcombe. Within 50 years this number rose to 860. After the First World War the population decreased; now it is on the increase again. Clean air, fertile soil, an excellent school, two thriving small industries providing job opportunities, and the much hoped-for housing project will surely be instrumental in attracting more and more young families to Cutcombe.

Dinder 🦚

The little village of Dinder, with its 150 inhabitants, lies in the valley between Wells and Shepton Mallet. It is mentioned in the Domesday Book as Denrenn, meaning 'in a deep valley between high hills' – an apt description because the Doulting Water, or river Sheppey, rushes along one boundary, and the Mendip Hills rise steeply on either side.

It has been an agricultural village, and it is known that clothing was made here in the 18th century when there was a leather mill. An old forge provided services in the main street, in a house still bearing that name. Along this street the river has been partially diverted to form a wide leat of running water in which the village people could dip their buckets, and this makes a picturesque foreground for a row of 16th century gabled cottages and a former public house which still displays the sign of 'The Dragon on the Wheel', being the crest of the local squire. Two farm-houses and the Victorian school building also overlook the water.

The village has several beautiful buildings, mostly in pinkish-grey stone, including its 15th century church standing in the well kept churchyard from which the surrounding hills are well seen. The late Georgian manor with its bow front has graceful parkland, half of which has now been converted into a Garden Centre, bounded by the river. The last squire to live in the house was Admiral of the Fleet Sir James Somerville who died there in 1947. Behind the church stands a Queen Anne house with handsome shell hood over the door. This decorative feature may commemorate the pilgrims who once passed by on their way from Winchester to Glastonbury, as there is a well in the orchard where, tradition says, they used to wash their feet before passing the night at a very old neighbouring cottage believed to have been the resthouse.

Church life had its special flavour in Victorian times. When Squire

Somerville paid the estate staff every Friday he would ask each man whether he had been to church the previous Sunday. The answer 'Yes' earned the man an extra half-crown. The fortunate recipients were known in the village as 'half-crown Christians'.

Many changes have come about since the last war with newcomers now contributing greatly to the life and activities here; but two farms and several cottages are still rented to people working on the land.

Ditcheat

Ditcheat derives from 'Dices-yat' or 'Dyke-gate', related to the regulation of rising water by lock-gate. It is an ancient agricultural village which has several interesting buildings. The church has Norman foundations and there is an interesting interior wall painting of St Christopher, probably 15th century.

In the late 16th century there appeared in London a religious tract entitled 'A true and most dreadful discourse of a woman possessed of the Devill, who in the likeness of a headless Beare, fetched her from out of her Bedd and in the presence of seven persons most strangely rolled her through the chambers and doune a high pair of stairs on the fower and twentieth of May last, 1584 at Dichet in Somersetshire'.

This unpleasant experience befell Margaret Cooper, wife of Stephen, a member of the rich and influential farming Coopers, who owned much land in Ditcheat and surrounding parishes. They lived somewhere near the church and manor house. Margaret made a good recovery from her harrowing experience, and was later interviewed by 'Master Doctor Coltington, Parson, of the same town'.

Ditcheat's most famous son is undoubtedly William Kingston who was born without arms. He was featured in the Bristol Mercury in 1826, where he was quoted as being 'a remarkable instance of the power of habit to remedy the defects of nature' for he was able to do with his feet that for which most people need hands! He could shave, write a bold, legible hand, and do all farm work, including saddling a horse. He was also a good bowler and wrestler. He married twice, and at the second ceremony put the ring on his wife's finger and signed the register with his foot. In all, he fathered nine sons and three daughters.

Dowlish Wake

Dowlish Wake is an attractive village consisting of mainly stone houses, some of which are thatched. Although new houses have been built, the village is mainly unspoilt. Two small brooks run through the village and the packhorse bridge is of historic importance.

The church stands on the hill and overlooks the village. The list of rectors goes back to the 1100s. The church holds the tomb of John Hanning Speke, the explorer who discovered the source of the Nile. Dr Livingstone attended his funeral. The last Union Flag to fly in Ginga, Uganda was sent to hang in the church at the time of their Independence. The manor was held by the Speke family for nearly 500 years until 1920 when the estate was split up and sold.

There are three farms, The New Inn, a porcelain shop, and Perry's Cider Mills, where traditional cider is made and sold in a 16th century thatched barn, combined with a country-style shop.

Dulverton

Dulverton, the 'secret place', is the southern gateway to the Exmoor National Park. The parish covers 3,538 acres and includes the village of Battleton, Pixton Park and Hollam House. From earliest times it has been a resting place for travellers crossing the river Barle at this safe fording point, sheltered on three sides by steep wooded hills and by the defences of three Celtic hill forts.

It is a small place of attractive architectural scale, which retains a village atmosphere. It is based on a typically medieval plan of a triangular market place lined with shops, cottages, inns and an unusual first-floor Town Hall converted from an 18th century Market House, where twice-monthly community markets and a monthly auction are held. Dulverton has been a convenient market centre since 1306, when it was licensed to hold a weekly market and a three-day fair at All Saints-Tide. The woollen industry was thriving then. Over the centuries, the leat from the river Barle has powered four mills in the town. The Dulverton Laundry is now the principal employer in the locality. The interesting old Dulverton Workhouse, built in 1855, now houses the administrative headquarters of the Exmoor National Park Authority.

Today, Dulverton provides a wide range of services for the 1300 inhabitants of the parish as well as other moorland villages. Health, welfare and education are all looked after. Dulverton depends largely on its own resources for recreation and entertainment. There are football and cricket teams, a billiards and snooker club and local enthusiasm has funded the building of squash courts and aims to add a bowling green.

There are four churches in the parish – Anglican, Methodist, Congregational and Roman Catholic – which work well together. A residential Youth Centre owned by the Catholic Diocese is housed next to the Catholic church and is used by church groups and youth clubs from all over Somerset.

Efforts to attract enterprises to a small industrial site have languished and Dulverton has been forced to consider its future role. Extra-mural university classes on 'Developing Your Community' concluded that tourism offered almost the only way forward. This was followed by the publication in 1987 and wide distribution of the town's first publicity leaflet.

Dunster 🎗

Dunster is a very old village well known as one of the prettiest and most interesting places on Exmoor.

In the Domesday Records it is called 'Torre' and the prefix 'Dun' comes from an old Celtic word also meaning 'hill'.

In the old days it was self sufficient; a thriving market town with several mills grinding corn or making cloth known as 'Dunsters'. There were farms, vineyards and a small sea port, all dominated by the castle and its Lords, from the time of Aluric the Saxon to the Normans, de Mohun and Luttrell.

In 1274 a priory was established on the north side of the church consisting of a prior and four brothers. Part of the building still exists as two cottages. Water was supplied for the monks and their farm from St Leonard's Well which was dug out on the side of Grabhurst Hill. From here the water was taken to a well-head in Conduit Lane and from thence to the priory. The small round building covering the water can still be seen in the Lane. However, beware how you approach it as it is said that the Minehead Witch – Old Mother Leaky – lives there!

The monks still haunt their old farm. Several years ago two local ladies were walking home in the 'dimpsey'. As they passed the Tithe Barn and approached the Dovecote, a monk bearing two pails of milk suspended from a yoke, crossed the road in front of them and disappeared into the priory garden. They have refused to walk that way again!

Dunster Castle came into prominence in the Civil War. At first the Luttrells supported Parliament, but when the Royalists seemed to be gaining ground they changed sides. After Cromwell's Forces captured Taunton and Bridgwater they decided that a determined effort be made to capture Dunster Castle. Colonel Blake besieged the castle for 160 days. During this time many of the cottages were damaged. A cannonball made a hole, which can still be seen, in a beam in the Yarn Market, and more were found in the roof of the church. At last the defenders realised that further resistance was useless and they negotiated a surrender. They were allowed to march out with drums beating and flags flying and go peacefully to their homes.

Life was hard for the lowly villagers in early times. The Pack Horse Bridge was known as Gallox Bridge, leading to Gallox Hill, where stood the 'Gallox' or 'Gallows Oak' from which many a poor wretch was hanged for stealing. Sixty-five years ago an old man told his family story for the first time. His family was very poor and his mother stole food for them. His father was arrested for the crime and he took the blame, thinking that the children needed their mother. He expected to be sent to prison. Instead he was shipped on the last convict boat to Australia and never saw his family again.

The village scene is enlivened today by fairs and festivals, candle-light evenings and stag and fox hunts, and also by occasional ghost sightings!

Near to Dunster are the small villages of Carhampton and Wootton Courtenay. Carhampton's church is St John the Baptist, of beautiful red sandstone. It contains a magnificent screen, a Peter's pence chest, and a frieze of carved oak around the aisle. Marshwood farmhouse nearby has walls at the back which are 700 years old, a front room has an Elizabethan ceiling, and the porch has plasterwork of a similar age, removed from the room above.

Wootton Courtenay is near the highest point on Exmoor-Dunkery Beacon, from which, on a clear day, the Malvern Hills, 120 miles away can be seen. The Commons here were the last Parliamentary enclosure on Exmoor in 1872.

Durston 🎐

The sleepy little village of Durston (no post office, no pub) would hardly seem the setting for scandal. Yet this was the case many centuries ago.

In the 12th century the lord of the manor, William de Erlegh, gave land to found a house for Augustine canons. A few years later a 'violent altercation' resulted in the death of the canon's steward who happened to be a relative of William. King Henry II made an inquiry into the events, passed a sentence of outlawry on the canons and declared their house forfeit. However, the investigations turned up another shocking fact beside the murder – several of the houses of the same order, supposedly for men who had renounced all worldly pleasures, had a few 'sisters'! These were swiftly removed from their various houses to Buckland in Durston where they formed the only Sisterhood of the Hospital of St John of Jerusalem.

What was it like for these nuns, suddenly flung together away from all they knew to deepest Somerset, and suffering probable ignominy and innuendo? There were at least nine of them, from places as far away as Oxford, Norfolk and Middlesex. The first prioress was called Fina, and she governed the house strictly for the long period of 60 years. The records of the priory have frequent references to the virtue and good living of the nuns.

A hundred and fifty years later the Sisters had grown to 50 in number, and had a steward, two brothers as chaplains, and one secular chaplain to minister to their needs. Charters had granted the nuns rights to gather fuel in local woods, to pasture cattle on certain moors, and they had a dovecote and fishponds to supplement their diet. A hermitage was built near the Sister's church at Buckland.

At the Dissolution in the 16th century the priory numbers had fallen to 13 Sisters and the Prioress. The lands were split up and sold, with those in Durston forming a large farm.

Today the farm is still called Buckland, and a large Georgian house stands on the site of the priory. A few gravestones have been found, and many local fields still bear names which can be traced back to those centuries. A canal and railway have cut through the priory lands. Commuters and tourists speed past the site, only a few stop in the layby and perhaps wonder what the large ponds (still with swans!) beside the busy road are doing there.

Close to Durston is the growing village of Creech St Michael, which was once at the junction of the Chard canal and the Bridgwater and Taunton canal. The village has two bridges at either side of it, both very old, and both crossing the river Tone. The very pretty church of St Michael is 13th century.

East Brent

East Brent, with the two small villages of Badgeworth and Biddisham nearby, is situated at the northern edge of the Somerset Levels, east of Brent Knoll, which rises 500 feet above the plain and which has been used as a beacon in times of celebration and peril. The summit has recently been purchased by the National Trust, which has replanted many of the trees lost through Dutch Elm disease.

The other landmark by which East Brent is known is the unique war memorial which stands at the entrance to the village. It has four life-sized servicemen standing round the shaft, and has recently been restored by the Parish Council.

In this flat area, drainage has always been by ditches, or rhines, around the fields. In the 19th century, typhoid swept the village, due to the drinking of contaminated water. The vicar at that time, Archdeacon Dennison, collected the water from the Knoll into deep chambers cut from the clay, and fed it to lower levels over a series of large stone slabs. It would cascade over these like waterfalls, finding its level in a large pond, which still remains. The water was filtered and piped to stand-pipes around the village, for the people to collect it.

This same Archdeacon and his wardens began the 'Harvest Home' for which East Brent is famous. Following a procession to church for a thanksgiving service, a gargantuan meal is served to about 600 people in a marquee. Originally the meal was for men only, and it was paid for by public subscription. The menu was (and still is) roast beef, Christmas pudding, bread, cheese and cider. Women and children received a free ham tea, there were steam roundabouts and dancing into the night. It is still a great day in East Brent, when scattered families re-unite, but now everything has to be paid for.

The same Archdeacon built a school beside the church, which he reserved for Anglican children! The non-conformists struck back, and built their own school. The second school was closed in 1973, and through the devoted work of a small committee, has been purchased, renovated, and become the focal point of the village.

The War Memorial at East Brent

Due to the proximity to good roads, East Brent is largely a dormitory village, but it also has a high proportion of residents who have retired. There is therefore a happy blend of people of varying backgrounds and interests. Village life is certainly changing, former cottages and farmhouses modernised to accommodate the incomers, and the quality of life is better than it has ever been.

East Chinnock

Midway between Yeovil and Crewkerne on the old turnpike road lies East Chinnock, a small community living at the bottom of the south slope of Chinnock Hill. Springs of pure water run from numerous sources, and even in the drought of 1976 they did not slacken. Rising from the village are delightful walks, some through sandy banks, where trees meet overhead and wild life is abundant.

The oldest building is the church, which guards the eastern approach to the village. It has greatly changed over the nine centuries since it was first granted to the Montacute Monastery. The chancel and font survive from Norman times, and the tower from the 15th century. During the 19th century, to accommodate the expanding population, alterations had to be made to the nave, doubling its width to the north. The church is acoustically excellent, so gaining for itself a reputation in choral singing.

East Chinnock remained as a possession of the Montacute Monastery until 1538, when Henry VIII confiscated it. In 1595 the Great Tithes passed to Corpus Christi College, Cambridge in whose hands they are still held. Five years later the manor was purchased by Henry Portman, and it remained in that lineage until 1924, when it was broken down into lots and sold, mostly to sitting tenants.

East Chinnock has never had a resident Lord of the Manor, and this may, in part, account for the strong community spirit which it has. The villagers have had to band together and appeal to authorities outside the village in order to settle internal disputes. Additionally it has been self-governing.

Until recent years the majority of East Chinnockians have earned their livings from agriculture. It is interesting that most of the farmsteads are in the village centre and their land is scattered, some on the high ground and some on the valley. There was an equal number of arable and grassland plots, and orchards and plantations as well. Today these have disappeared and the parish is again arable and grassland, with the addition of three specialist farms, a piggery, a poultry farm and a horticultural centre. No longer does farming need a large workforce so the majority of the villagers have to go to neighbouring towns to earn their living.

There are no grand residences in East Chinnock, but there are examples of solid 17th century cross-passage houses, and one, the finest, Weston House goes back further, to medieval times. The Portman estate built extensively in the 19th century, and Barrows, a superior farmhouse is probably the best of these. Of the 20th century several small groups of houses have been built of differing designs, all of which add to the individuality and character of the village.

East Coker 🌿

East Coker is a village of thatched Hamstone cottages with some modern infilling, of farms, a small Council Estate and two modern housing development areas. A new village hall built in the late 1970s is one of the modern amenities, situated near open fields beyond the site of the old Webbing Factory and the Saw Mills. The population is approximately 2000. Although situated 2½ miles from the A30 it is still a true village with a church, manor house, pub, village green, school, post office and shop.

The many Hamstone cottages of the old village cluster around the church of St Michael and All Angels on a hill by the manor house, with the paddock and adjacent almshouses built by Archdeacon Helyar in 1640.

The settlements at Burton and North Coker are now part of East Coker. The school built in 1851, now extended and modernised has 250 children on the roll from the surrounding areas.

At Burton there is a row of cottages once built as the Workhouse on the site of an old chantry around 1550, with another group at Garden Row of more recent date, which housed the gardening staff from North Coker House.

Hymerford House, a large thatched house of Tudor origin, much altered and restored since 1651 when it was the birth-place of William Dampier, navigator, geographer and buccaneer, who first mapped part of the coast of Australia. Paviott's Mill, a three-storey brick Tudor building

The village post office and stores at East Coker

with many original features still visible where Cromwell is said to have stabled his horses.

Three mills operated from the same stream at Holywell (Hew Hill), East Coker Mill and Paviott's Mill. Flax was grown in many areas until the late 1800s. Nearly every cottage had its looms for the weaving of

Coker cloth. The Twine and Webbing Mills were founded by Mr Felix Drake in 1872 using local skills and continued for over 100 years. Ropes and webbing from Messrs Drake & Co were used in the ascent of Mt Everest by Sir Edmund Hillary and also to lower Sir Winston Churchill's coffin at his interment. The Saw Mills were founded in 1880 by Joseph Perry to service the looms, his invention the Twine Twisting Machinery, reached manufacturers throughout England and Northern Ireland. The company sadly closed in 1979. The site now contains several small industrial units, some operated by local people including a sign-writer, printer and engineer.

Comparatively few residents were born in the village, but there are still some old family names – Boucher, Stagg, Dodge that appear many times in church records and whose descendants still live in East Coker. The Boucher family dates back 600 years.

T. S. Eliot's ancestor, Andrew Eliot, born in 1627, emigrated to America from Coker. Eliot visited East Coker in 1936–37 and published his poem entitled *East Coker* as part of his *Quartet*. His ashes are interred at St Michael's church and a memorial tablet was erected in 1965.

East Huntspill

There has been a settlement in East Huntspill since Roman times. Farming has been the main occupation of the community and many of the farms date from the late 1700s. There was a hamlet in Katherine Street dating from 1790, and consisting of three houses. It is situated 1½ miles north east of the church. At the south end of the village there is another hamlet called Cote, where there are a few farms and cottages.

The parish church was at West Huntspill, but in 1840 a new one was built at East Huntspill, and was known as a Chapel of Ease, thus making it more convenient for the parishioners not to have to undertake the long walk if they had no means of riding to their Sunday worship. Five years later the Ecclesiastical Parish was divided, and became a separate entity. The Parish is now united again, with the Rector living at West Huntspill, and serving both churches.

A school was built, about 1895, with a house for the headmaster, in New Road. The original one was next to the church, and is now the parish hall which is used for meetings of all kinds.

Part of the village is called Bason Bridge and the railway ran through there from Highbridge to Glastonbury. The line was used by the milk factory which was opened in 1909 by the Wilts United Dairies and later taken over by Unigate, finally closing in 1984.

East Huntspill is well-known for the Annual Harvest Home celebrations which date from 1910. At one time these would have taken the form of games by the river, but now it is a much more elaborate event, starting with a service of Thanksgiving in the church, followed by a luncheon attended by several hundred people, tea and a funfair for the children.

One of the oldest farms in the area, New Road Farm, has now started a new project, collecting unusual birds and animals. It is open to the public and has created a new interest particularly popular with school parties.

East Quantoxhead & Kilve ❧

East Quantoxhead is a picturesque village, much of which overlooks a central millpond. The Court House is the seat of the Luttrell family, resident in this area since the time of Domesday. They were largely responsible for the church of St Mary as it stands today.

Before the village hall was built in 1913, Band of Hope meetings and Penny Readings were held in the old Dame School which had become redundant when the new school was built in 1890.

There used to be in the village, a builder, a wheelwright, blacksmith, general shop, shoemaker and cobbler, laundry, miller and baker. The three farms used to have 20 cart horses and employ about 20 men. Today there are no working horses and only 8 men.

Many people can remember that in Kilve forty years ago it was possible to stroll down the middle of the road from Hilltop Hamlet to the village: now it is the main A39. There were still, then, four shops and a mill grinding animal feed. In earlier days William Wordsworth walked on 'Kilve's smooth shore by the green sea' where the Chantry stood. Founded in 1329 by Sir Simon de Furneaux, now it is a ruin, burned in 1850 by a fire which flamed brightly, they say, fuelled by the kegs of smuggled brandy stored there.

Gone forever is the blacksmith's forge which stood where today's bakery is and where, perhaps, the smugglers' horses were shod – those same horses who were trained to gee-up when the Excise men shouted whoa! No toll-house now, in the centre of the village, but a car park where it stood until the middle of this century, and no chapel, but still the village hall, a monument to the memory of England's longest reigning Queen.

Edington 🌿

Edington is one of the string of villages along the Poldens which had early connections with Glastonbury Abbey. A Holy Well by the roadside below the church can still be seen, its waters springing from the clays of lower lias providing water rich in minerals reputed to have healing powers.

The larger houses such as Edington Manor, Edington House and the Great House provided work for the women and girls 'in service', whilst the farms, including those of Edington Manor estate, needed the men as farm and estate workers. Many of the farms have survived, although few now employ hired labour.

Scything hay and corn was a task continued all summer before machinery took over, and bands of mowers would move from farm to farm as they were needed, sleeping out in barns or under hedges until the job was done, sometimes reaching as far as the Mendips across the moor where several hay crops were taken from the meadows. Each band would work under a captain who gave the time, and the rest had to follow him, keeping time like rowers in a boat, working on the condition that there was a good supply of cider – but they never got drunk because they sweated so much!

Stone was quarried in local fields and the harder blue lias was dressed and used for building by village stonemasons. Softer white lias stone was quarried near Landshire Farm (Chilton Polden) for the cement works at Puriton. As the work was seasonal, some men used to go to Wales for the winter to work in the mines, returning in spring in time for hoeing and road mending (each parish being responsible for its own roads at that time).

The footpath which meanders from the church in Burtle to St George's, Edington, now called the Church Path, used to be known as the Burial Path. In winter months, Burtle church, being on low ground, had problems. As a grave was being dug, it would fill with water very quickly, thus making it impossible to complete digging for interment. So the deceased was carried to Edington for burial, where, as the churchyard is on a hillside, no similar problems occurred. Sometimes the moor between

76

the two villages would be flooded, so the coffin had to be taken part of the way by boat. Nowadays the moors are well drained by pumping stations.

Edithmead 🎐

Edithmead, a small hamlet numbering less than 200 persons, is situated between the A38 – the original turnpike road – and Burnham-on-Sea. Its dwellings, mostly farms and cottages with a sprinkling of newer housing, cluster either side of the village road.

It has been said that the village derived its name from Queen Edith, wife of Edward the Confessor, and there is evidence that this lady did have estates in Somerset.

The little tin-clad mission church of St Andrew was brought to the village in 1919. This building, when consecrated, took the place of the railway carriage where all church services had previously been held. This railway carriage was situated in the doctor's garden and the particular plot where it stood was called Chapel Ground, and was very stony and hard to dig.

Before the last war, on sunny afternoons, the quiet road from Burnham-on-Sea resounded to the clip-clop of horses hooves, as the hired open carriage with a coachman in top hat drove well-to-do elderly ladies into the countryside to take the air.

Drinking water was dipped from the big rhine which flowed through the village, or if you were one of the lucky ones from your own well. After an old tramp had been found dead, floating in the rhine close to where water was dipped, villagers insisted on having a piped water supply. This supply was referred to for many years as 'a drop of Axbridge'.

In 1841 the main Great Western Railway line from Paddington to Penzance was built through the northern pastures and gave birth to the two deep ponds and their teeming wildlife which have always been such a feature of the village.

Now sadly, many of the old farmhouses have been pulled down and the space infilled with modern bungalows. One such farm site now houses a huge trailer and caravan park.

After hundreds of years of tranquillity and obscurity, Edithmead suddenly achieved a dubious kind of fame by becoming one of the many interchanges on the M5 motorway. The coming of the motorway, in addition to taking many acres of farmland to the south, occasioned a wide slip road to Burnham-on-Sea being built across pastures in the centre of the village, intersecting the original road, and completely changing the little hamlet.

Enmore 🌿

The village of Enmore lies at the foot of the Quantock Hills about three miles west of Bridgwater. The ancient name of Animere in the Domesday Book means 'duck pool' – perhaps the small lake in front of the castle. This stands on the site of the manor house given, with its lands, to William Malet by William the Conqueror, and held by his family for centuries.

Nearby is the early English church dedicated to St Michael. It has a Norman doorway whose rounded arch of yellowed stone displays double dog-tooth ornamentation. The Malet Hatchment on the west wall shows detail of the Malet family from 1100–1681. Nearby hang two Malet helmets of early times. The peal of six bells in the tower is no longer rung regularly. The tenor bell bears the inscription:

> To the Grave He summons all
> To the Church the living call.

The village school has a claim to fame in the annals of education. Known as Enmore National School it was the first free elementary school in the country, founded in 1810 by the Rev John Poole who was rector of Enmore for 61 years. He built his rectory on glebe land at some distance from the church. Wordsworth, Coleridge and Southey, with his cousin Tom Poole, came to visit from Nether Stowey. Named Poole House, it is now divided into three dwellings.

The post office and general shop is lodged in the old bakery. Here the family of Collard handed their business from father to son for almost four hundred years.

Two inns in the village each have a skittle alley with the nine pins and three heavy wooden balls. Enmore Inn is in Lower Enmore and from there the road rises to the Tynte Arms.

An 18 hole golf course has been made in Enmore Park. It has a strong membership. The ancient British packway from Watchet to Bridgwater, which skirts the village, can be seen clearly as it crosses the course. Near

The Norman doorway of Enmore church

the clubhouse on the main road is the village hall. Named the Memorial Hall it was built to commemorate the 1914–18 war. Many social events take place here, the Annual Flower show being a popular event.

Evercreech

The Parish is first mentioned in 1066 in a charter drawn up by Edward the Confessor as being the possession of the Bishop of Wells. It is also mentioned in the Domesday survey of 1084–86.

St Peter's church is mentioned in 1178, but not the church as it is today which is notable for its painted roof and ring of 10 bells, often visited by teams of ringers during the summer months. Along the south side of the church (outside) there are three gargoyles, executed in stone by a carver from Wells in 1842.

While doing the work he lodged in the village and not being very good tempered he fell out with the vicar, quarelled with the publican and two women gossips also annoyed him. When the work was finished, he invited the people he had lodged with to view his handiwork, pointing out the 'portraits' – the parson (a hideous monster), the publican (a monkey) and the two women (two cats).

The village cross is approximately 15th century and originally stood in the churchyard. It is a prayer cross and was moved to the village green in 1781, such crosses were used by travelling preachers and for public proclamations.

There are records of a silk mill in Evercreech in 1801 where about 100 children worked and lived, most of whom were paupers and apprenticed to the master of the mill, some being as young as 8 or 9. There have also been a rope works and mineral water works in the village.

Many people may only have heard of Evercreech in connection with the railway which passed through it – The Somerset and Dorset Railway which amalgamated with the Somerset Central Railway about 1859, originally laid from Wimborne to Glastonbury, later the main line being extended to Evercreech and up to Bath.

Today the main source of employment is the Unigate factory, there is also a new industrial site being developed which already houses a thriving haulage firm. New housing is also being built on several sites.

Nearby is the permanent site of the Royal Bath & West showground and the considerable permanent infrastructure that this provides is sometimes used for local events.

Exton & Bridgetown 🌿

These two hamlets are individually so small that they are usually spoken of in the same breath. Exton is situated up a steep hill while Bridgetown is down below, beside the river Exe. Thence Essetune (the enclosure on the river Esse) and Rigge (as it was known in Norman England) from which presumably Riggetune (or Bridgetown) was derived. There are several very old buildings, the most important being St Peter's church, Exton. Parts of the building date back to the 13th century and some herring-bone masonry indicates building of the Norman period.

The Badgers Holt, formerly known as The Rock Inn, is an ancient Exmoor Hostelry where the local cricket teams gather on summer evenings. Just across the river Exe lies the ground of the local cricket club, founded by Mr Roy Nesfield in 1924, a great enthusiast of the game who passed on his interest to the villagers and taught them to play. He donated a thatched pavilion where teas are still served.

In the early 1900s the Bridgetown Band would celebrate Bridgetown Club Day by leading all the parishioners up to Exton church for a service. Being a 1 in 4 hill it was quite a climb! They all wore green sashes and carried red peonies which were the Bridgetown colours, most people grew their own peonies especially for this day. This annual event took place on 1st June but sadly in the early 1920s it faded out.

In the early 1900s Bridgetown Mill was in full working order, owned by the Phillips family, who employed a number of villagers. Now no longer used as a mill it is a very pleasant caravan park.

Before the rock that gave its name to The Rock Inn was demolished, the main coachroad to Dulverton traversed the Exe from east to west rather than north to south as now. The old bridge across the Exe is still there as is the forge which used to serve the horses, although the building is now used to mend horticultural machinery.

Fiddington 🌿

Fiddington is a scattered rural community set in gently undulating farmland of 1,314 acres. The church, with the village hall beside it, holds a central position within the parish. These are set back from the road, with green fields to the north and west and the playing field, bounded by a spinney and the brook, to the south of them.

The houses in nearby Church Road make up the actual village. These are in a variety of building materials and sizes, some fronted by walled gardens, some hidden by shrubs and two sited end-on to the highway.

Celtic peoples used the river Parrett, Pedride they called it, as a defensive boundary between their own lands and those of the West Saxons. After they were defeated late in the 7th century, this area was incorporated in the Saxon administration system and Fiddington became a part of the Hundred of Cannington.

The Saxons were democratic people and Fiddington, the Tun of Fita's people, would have had its Moot, equivalent to a Parish Council. The Moot appointed ten men to be responsible for law and order, the head of whom was the Tythingman. In Fiddington is the long established field name of Tythingman's Close. Did the inhabitants put aside this 3 acre field for the benefit of their head 'policeman'?

The church of St Martin of Tours was built in the early 14th century. Saxon herring-bone masonry and a Celtic carving on a reddish sandstone quoin in the fabric of the building, point to the possibility of an earlier church. Recent studies suggest that the grotesque sexual nature of the Celtic carving, known as a Sheila-na-Gig, was intended to deter devils and evil doers.

The village school, built in 1891 was once a centre for the education of 85 children, some of whom walked there from outside the parish. The school had been built on land belonging to Manor Farm and Mr A W Meaker donated it as a village hall when the school closed in 1954. Later the Benjamin Meaker Trust made possible the purchase of the playing field.

Fivehead ༼

The village of Fivehead lies on the southern slope of the Curry Rivel Ridge. It is bordered on the south side by the Isle river and the Rag (or Fivehead) river, and on the north by the chequered counterpane of Sedgemoor. The moors were not drained and fenced until after the 1820 Enclosure Acts, and so access to the village was difficult for many centuries. Fivehead has developed very slowly indeed since pre-Saxon times. The name is a corruption of Five Hydes, a hyde being 120 acres of land.

Life in the village proceeded at a very leisurely pace until the 18th century, when at the Earl of Chatham's instigation a turnpike road was cut from Langport to Red Post. As travelling became easier, development was speeded up. The building of a sewage works in the mid 20th century made many more houses possible and expansion became faster still.

The village already has an excellent bakery, a thriving shop and post office, a first class hostelry 'The Crown', a foundry which has replaced both old forges, a large chicken hatchery, a lively WI and a play school firmly established in the old Victorian schoolhouse. This has been refurbished to provide a village hall. The most amazing metamorphosis of all has been the music-recording studio which has been established at the lovely old Manor of Cathanger. This imposing house has been in continuous occupation, though with varying fortunes, since the Norman Conquest.

The marshy nature of the land surrounding the village made withies and teazels a natural crop in both parishes, and although withies have suffered the competition of imported baskets, teazels are still grown here commercially.

The Norman church of St Martin's stands next to the war memorial on the village green, and contains many old tombs and stained glass windows. It was one of the few churches in Somerset that could not afford a bible when after the Restoration in 1660 a bible was compulsory in every church in the land.

There is an old Coaching Drove running along the northern parish boundary where an occasional apple, pear or plum tree marks the sites of domestic settlements, long since gone. There are a few farms along this drove whose adzed ceiling joists and cruck beams are clear evidence of their ancient origin, for cruck beams were discontinued in the 14th century, and roofs began to be supported by walls as they are today. This drove leads to Langport, past the Heronry at Swell and the RSPB bird-sanctuary in Fivehead woods.

Goathurst & Halswell

Goathurst, lying 4 miles south-west of Bridgwater is described in the Domesday Book. Half a mile up the hill from the village is Halswell House, always a separate manor, also mentioned in Domesday. The manor of Halswell by the 14th century was in the hands of the Halswell family; in the course of time the Halswells intermarried with three other prominent families, the Tyntes of Chelvey, the Kemys of Cefn Mably and the Whartons, originally from Westmoreland.

Sir Halswell Tynte who built the present Halswell House in 1689 was the son of Jane Halswell and John Tynte.

In the 17th century the Halswell family bought the manor of Goathurst, thus uniting the manors of Goathurst and Halswell.

The family succeeded in 1916 in claiming the barony of Wharton and it was this Lord Wharton and his wife who established the pattern of life in Goathurst until the death of Lady Wharton. Since then the main house has been divided into flats and the ballroom used as a furniture depository.

According to the historian Nicholaus Pevsner, Halswell House was once the foremost House in Somerset.

Since the Second World War, the gardens had been largely taken over by nature and the whims of a variety of occupants. But now there is a new resident owner well qualified to make an integrated garden from its disparate parts. Mr J Tuckey has been a Gold Medallist Exhibitor at Chelsea Flower Show, and he hopes to have the grounds of Halswell available for public viewing and enjoyment in 1989, a mammoth task after years of neglect.

Hambridge & Westport ෨ℰ෩

There is much to be done in an English garden in the autumn and at the turn of the century it was not unusual to hear a happy gardener singing as he gathered the fruits of his labours. In 1903 a certain John England was in good voice with the song *The Seeds of Love* as he worked in the grounds of the vicarage. The vicar's house guest at the time was the renowned Cecil Sharp. The incident was to have a lasting effect on British music for it inspired Sharp to lead the folksong revival in England and it started his collection of songs. A plaque outside the old vicarage (now a nursing home) records the event, the plaque having been erected in 1961 at a ceremony attended by Sharp's daughters.

Hambridge and Westport had a direct link with the Bristol Channel via the river at Bridgwater and in those Victorian days the newly-constructed Westport canal did a flourishing trade. This answers the question why so many properties were built in Bridgwater red brick when the favoured building material was the true Somerset grey stone or the honey-coloured Hamstone. Today the only traces of the canal are where it runs alongside the road through Westport and by the two large warehouse buildings standing derelict at the canal basin.

Aubrey Keep 1983

The old brewery and mill building at Hambridge (illustration by Aubrey Keep of Ilminster is reproduced by kind permission of the Chard and Ilminster News)

The local brewery, mentioned in the Domesday Book, ceased to trade in the 1970s. The delightful brewery and mill building still stands and is now home for a firm making quality furniture.

The brewery and flour mills stood at the lower end of the village close by the river Isle and when the road flooded, and that was frequently, a local carter would ferry children to school by horse and cart at a penny a time!

The water and the land combined to help the local economy with the growth of withies for the flourishing basket-making trade. This still continues and has been joined by a newer craft – the re-caning of chairs and other furniture.

Throughout the years the people of Hambridge and Westport have been a united ambitious community and they have the evidence to prove it. Close to the memorial honouring the dead of two world wars stands the Royal British Legion hut. It was bought for £100 and transported by voluntary labour from Salisbury Plain just after the First World War. Today it has been almost pensioned off by an even bolder piece of village enterprise, a brand new hall that won the Somerset Village Ventures award.

Hardington Mandeville 🐾

Hardington Mandeville is in south Somerset, some four miles south-west of Yeovil and only a mile or two from the Dorset border. The name Hardington is Anglo-Saxon and means 'the settlement of Hearda's people'. In 1086, Domesday Book recounts, the manor belonged to the King, who later handed it over to Geoffrey de Mandeville.

Hardington has always been a farming community. Today there are under 600 inhabitants, but the number of homes has risen considerably. Now there are some 10 farms engaged mainly in dairying, with some arable and sheep, as well as a large nursery.

Hardington is divided into three main parts. The largest is usually referred to as 'the Mandeville', and contains the church, the Mandeville Arms public house (with a skittle alley in its grounds, for this is the heart of Somerset skittles country) and the High Street (which has no shops!). Next, down in the valley of the Chinnock Brook to the north, is Hardington Moor, where there is another pub, the Royal Oak (again with skittle alley) and the village shop and post office. Finally, about a mile away to the south, in the Broad river valley, is Hardington Marsh, a handful of farms and dwellings down a 'no through road', which always seems very remote and quiet.

St Mary's church, Hardington, stands in a commanding position with fine views northwards across the valley to Coker Hill and westwards towards the Quantocks and other West Somerset hills. There was probably a Saxon church on the site which the Normans chose – the base of a Saxon preaching cross can still be seen in the churchyard. The medieval church was largely re-built in the 19th century, but part of the Norman tower remains.

Near the church is the former school, which closed in about 1960 and now forms the village hall. Among other village activities there is an annual gymkhana, and hounds meet at the Royal Oak several times a year.

Until about the 1920s most of the land, along with property in adjoining parishes, was owned by Viscount Portman. Since the Second World War, many new houses and bungalows have been built, often on land which was previously occupied by cider apple orchards. This is all infilling along the roads and has not increased the inhabited area much.

Haselbury Plucknett

To the casual observer Haselbury Plucknett is an unremarkable village. It has none of the attractions which would tempt the speeding tourists to make a diversion from the A30 just to look at it. It was not always so apparently unremarkable. For several centuries it was an important place of pilgrimage, visited by many important people, including two kings.

The Domesday book records the village as Halberge, held by a Saxon Thane Brismar. (It acquired its suffix later, when it was held by Alan de Plugenet.). There was already a church of St Michael and All Angels on the same site as the present one, and it was to this church that the visitors and pilgrims came to seek help and advice from St Wulfric. He took up residence here, as an anchorite early in the 12th century, occupying a cell on the site of the present vestry, and those who sought his help had to knock on his window and converse with him through that window.

He led a physically uncomfortable life wearing chainmail next to his skin and a hair shirt, sleeping on a rough hurdle, and dependent for his sustenance on the offerings of the community. Even in this he was frugal, eating only bread or porridge, and drinking only water except on certain feast days when he allowed himself to take a little wine.

At that time an anchorite was an important person in the community dispersing help, advice and counselling and sometimes reprimands. Wulfric spent much time in prayer and contemplation and also wrote books for use in the church.

Wulfric also had the gift of prophecy and he correctly foretold the death of Henry I, which happened whilst the king was on a visit to France. He also foretold that his own death would bring about strife over the burial of his body. Sure enough, various religious establishments wished to claim the remains but Wulfric had expressed a wish to be buried at Haselbury so all the claims were resisted. However it was thought necessary to move the body several times to avoid the possibility of theft, and now nobody knows where exactly his body lies. It may be under the present church, or outside in the churchyard along with those of lesser mortals.

Hatch Beauchamp

The village lies east of the Blackdowns, between Taunton and Ilminster. It is dominated by Hatch Court, built on the site of the Beauchamp family's Norman manor house. The church is situated within the park and was thoroughly restored in 1867.

In 1907 Emily Dibble wrote a diary. She lived with her aunt and uncle at Capland Farm and her diary gives a vivid picture of a way of life now gone forever.

By the time she was 20 she was a skilful home-maker, very much involved in the life of the farm, her family, the chapel and neighbours (one of whom she was to marry some years later). She had all the traditional skills, making and 'printing' butter (often over 30lb in a day), rearing ducks, bantams, chicks and turkeys, buying preserving sugar from Mr Smallridge's shop for her gooseberry jam and pies, and going daily to buy a paper from Mr Tytherleigh.

When 700 sheep arrived in the night it was Emily who got up to look after the drovers, without complaint. She gives an impression of living well as everything came into season on their land. She looked after sick or injured farm-hands, changing dressings or perhaps making 'a brew of elder blossom tea'.

Chapel was an important focus in her life. She went three times on Sundays and 'helped with the children's band', where the behaviour was always recorded as 'very bad indeed'. She managed better with the bells, copying out music for them, but was often 'stiff from their use' the next day.

Emily Dibble lived on in the village until she was 84.

Hemington

Hemington lies in a quiet valley set below the junction of two ancient roads, one along which the Roman general Vespasian led his army, the other travelled by pilgrims making their way to Wells and Glastonbury. Its name is of Saxon origin, probably the settlement of a chieftain called Hemm or Hemma.

The Lord of the Manor who inherited in 1776 was Sir Charles Bamfylde who was famous for his debts, perhaps because he was a friend of the then Prince of Wales. This condition made a strong impact on Hemington as he chopped down all the trees to raise money to pay his debts.

Fame, or perhaps notoriety touched it in 1740 when the occupants of a nearby farmhouse, still standing in almost its original state, a Madam Elizabeth Branch and her daughter were convicted of having 'barbarously put to death beneath their roof an unfortunate servant girl'. Strange lights were seen to flicker across her grave in Hemington churchyard and those who had so wronged her were hanged at Ilchester the following May. The legend of the haunted churchyard lingers on.

Hemington has a small, simple, beautiful church, its churchyard lovingly tended. A cascade beside the road is called the 'waterfall' by the children and edged with flowers in the spring. Perhaps Hemington's most significant building is now a dilapidated farm shed with planning permission for conversion to a bungalow. Old inhabitants still refer to it as the 'Laundry'. It was in fact a communal laundry beside the stream and an elderly lady in her nineties who died recently could remember using it. Is it coincidence do you think that until recently parts of a neighbouring garden were covered with soapwort?

On the first weekend of July the road is closed and the gardens are thrown open to the public. From car parks at either end a growing number of people visit these and the many stalls. One house provides strawberry teas and a horse drawn carriage provides transport. It has become an annual event not only because the money is needed for the upkeep of the church but because so much community spirit is engendered. The hard work becomes worthwhile and the pleasure of residents and visitors is making Hemington Open Weekend a must for many from near and far.

High Ham 🐏

The hill on which High Ham stands was, in centuries past, an island rising out of water and marshland. The hamlets of Henley and Low Ham hide within the skirts of the hill whilst the lower slopes of the escarpment are clothed with the woods of Aller and Beer. There has been a settlement in this place for hundreds of years and in Domesday Book, the parish was referred to as Hame.

In the centre of the village lies the green surrounded by tall trees and a group of listed buildings, the 15th century church and an Elizabethan schoolhouse built in 1598 by Adrian Schael, the Rector of High Ham. The village church of St Andrew has a beautiful rood screen and, on the outside, a row of amusing figures depicting a trumpeter, fiddler, piper and a monkey nursing a baby. At a little distance from the village there is a thatched cap windmill now owned and maintained by the National Trust.

High Ham is still very much a farming community. The farms, particularly in Low Ham and Henley are on the main village roads with their fields dispersed over a wider area of moorland and hillside. Sheep and cattle are driven to pasture on the Levels where the grass is lush and green. The people who own and work the farms are proud, independent and hard-working, bearing names that have been known in these parts for generations.

Until comparatively recent years the place was largely self-supporting with all the usual village shops and amenities and a very active local life. Sadly with changing shopping habits there is now only one shop and a post office which opens three half-days a week. However, the milkman and baker still deliver and on some days a mobile shop calls. The church is active and the village hall Committee organise several functions, while a new school is being built.

Hinton St George

Hinton St George is a perfect village, home of the Poulette family since the 15th century. The Duke of Monmouth came here during his 1685 Rebellion, and Elizabeth Parcet touched him for the King's Evil.

Hinton House was the home of the Pouletts, and there are a large number of monuments to members of the family in the parish church of St George.

Holcombe

Holcombe has an interesting association with Captain Robert Falcon Scott, the Antarctic explorer, who was brought up at the manor. His parents are buried at the old church, and his name also is on their memorial. The senior citizens' complex called Scotts Close was opened by his son, Peter Scott, some years ago.

Holcombe old church is fascinating, with a minstrel's gallery and no electricity. It is 1½ miles from the village, as the whole village was moved away from the 'Combe' when the plague struck. The survivors built afresh on the top of the hill. One of the local pubs is known as the Ring of Roses, from the old children's rhyme which describes the fate of plague victims.

Horrington

Horrington – Horningdun – the place of the hill like a horn – is dominated by the Mendips, on the southern slopes of which it lies, two or three miles above Wells. With Pen Hill (1000 feet) on its north-west border, West Horrington clings along the slope of the hill, while East Horrington has Masbury Castle, crowned by its Iron Age hill fort, to the north-east. To reach either village from Wells one rises about 500 feet so the views across Somerset are tremendous.

The two villages, though they share a name, have different characteristics. West Horrington has been involved in lead mining and some of the cottages have the remains of a one-man pit behind the house. Once the lead near the surface was worked out, the pits were abandoned and in the

91

19th century the occupations of the villagers were mainly in farming, quarrying and road mending.

East Horrington seems to have been always a farming village. Many of the farms began to disappear in Victorian times as the smaller ones became too small and their fields were bought up by their larger neighbours. Their farmhouses and cottages scattered throughout the parish are now lived in by people working in Wells and further afield and by retired folk.

There has been some new house building since 1945 at a pace which has allowed both villages to keep their identity rather than to become just dormitories, which is fortunate considering the lack of a central meeting place. There is now no pub in the villages, though there used to be several, the only survivor being Slab House on the Bath road. The 1839 church was closed in 1977, when the parish was joined with St Thomas's, Wells. The old schoolroom in East Horrington was a place for get-togethers until it became too dilapidated. The present school, opened in 1897, is nicely placed between the two villages and in some ways acts as a village hall.

For the past 140 years many villagers have been employed at the Mendip Hospital, which lies within the parish. In its early days as a County Asylum, it was more like a village with its own farm, gardens, workshops, and a large staff. The patients often took their walks round Horrington, were accepted well and helped when necessary. This contact has been strengthened during the past thirty years by the Friends of the Hospital.

Horton & Broadway ✤

In days gone by the countryside around Horton and Broadway came within the boundary of the Royal Forest of Neroche. By Tudor times cultivation of the forest and common land had begun and farmhouses were built, several of which still stand today although, of course, altered in the passage of time.

The original hamlet of Horton is now referred to as Horton Cross. The more recent Horton village grew around a scattering of dwellings which were erected as the common land was gradually cleared in the area remembered as Broadway Hill. In the early 19th century the roadway through the village (now the A303) was considerably improved and it became part of the new coaching route from Devonport to London.

The church of St Peter, built of stone with Bath stone dressings, was consecreated in 1900 and continued the work of the old Mission room. The Wesleyan Chapel was built in 1833, the school followed in 1877 with places for a maximum of 80 children who were excused from attending on local fair days or for farm work, including teazling – teazles were supplied to the cloth-making industry and crops were grown in this area until fairly recently.

Broadway takes its name from its situation, being built along the ancient broad path leading into the Forest of Neroche. A number of beautiful high grade 16th and 17th century houses are to be found in the village, Porch House being the oldest with pre-Tudor origins.

The parish church, built of stone in the early English and perpendicular style with an embattled tower, is dedicated to St Aldhelm and St Eadburga and stands well away from the rest of the village. The reason for this is unknown.

The villages of Horton and Broadway are separated by the river Ding which provides a natural boundary, but five road bridges over this little river make it easy for inhabitants on both sides to share facilities – and indeed the vicar, who serves both churches.

Huish Episcopi

Huish Episcopi, commonly known as Huish until the 18th century is a large country parish of very irregular shape, surrounding Langport on three sides. Besides the actual village, which is near and around the church, it consists of three hamlets, Pibsbury, Wearne and Coombe.

By the end of the 12th century the 'Manor of Huish Episcopi' was controlled by the Bishop of Bath – hence Episcopi, ie of the Bishop.

The oldest surviving part of the church is the Norman doorway which shows signs of discolouration by fire, caused perhaps by the fire which destroyed the church in the 14th century. The beautifully proportioned tower, built of blue lias and Hamstone is the greatest attraction, and was depicted on a 9p postage stamp in 1972.

When walking the public footpaths it is not difficult to realise that farming and horticulture were once the main sources of employment in the parish. Since the end of the Second World War modern housing developments have steadily taken over the apple orchards and many of the cattle grazing pastures, while the village garden allotments have given way to a council housing estate.

Huish Episcopi once had a tannery which provided employment for local men. It ceased to operate in the early 1920s and remained unoccupied for some years. Eventually it was developed into a modern abattoir which has recently been extended.

Most of the older houses in the village and in the wider area of the parish are built of blue lias stone which was quarried locally, and it is interesting to note that, although no local stone is readily available at the present time, the modern houses are constructed of manufactured stone of the blue lias colour.

When education became compulsory a Board school was built in 1877 and is still in use today as Huish Episcopi Primary School. Recreation and extra educational facilities are available at the Comprehensive school which is situated near the church.

Houses with thatched roofs are now only few. There are two at Wearne, one at Pibsbury and three in Huish village, one of the three being the only remaining public house within the parish.

Keinton Mandeville ✍

The village of Keinton Mandeville lies on the former turnpike road which runs from Somerton to Castle Cary and then on to London via Salisbury. A well known local character in the 19th century, quarry owner Oliver Chalker, earned a reputation as 'The Strong Man of Keinton' and at the age of 91 was reputed to have pushed a wheelbarrow containing five hundredweights of local stone. As a boy he played with the most distinguished son of Keinton, John Henry Broadribb, born in 1838, who later became Sir Henry Irving, the greatest actor of his time.

Keinton Mandeville was first mentioned in the Domesday Book as Chintone, part of the manor of Bertone, now the neighbouring village of Barton St David. The subsequent Lord of the Manor was a descendant of Geoffrey de Mandeville who came to England with William the Conqueror.

Until recently the main activity in the village was the quarrying of its blue lias stone, used for ornamental work and building throughout Somerset. The large stone slabs, some seven feet high, referred to as the 'shields' are still much in evidence in and around the village today. One quarry remains active. The stone was formerly worked by hand and taken to Castle Cary station by horse and wagon. In the 1860s one of the quarries had a primitive railway with both sleepers and rails cut from the

The 'mop shaker' at Keinton Mandeville

blue lias stone. There were only two other similar trackways in the country, both in Devon.

The church of St Mary Magdalen is peacefully situated to the south of the village. It is a homely country church with a 13th century chancel and a simple Norman font. The church was partly rebuilt in 1800. Other 13th century architecture can still be found in the village, including a barn in Queen Street, the roof being a fine example of the Raised Cruck Design.

Before the Second World War there were no less than 15 shops in the village; only one third of these remain, plus two public houses, but the village retains a thriving school with increasing numbers of pupils. There is no longer a wheelwright or blacksmith's shop and lorries have replaced the horses and wagons which once moved the stone. Many of the cider orchards have now been developed but some still blossom and the character of the village and its inhabitants remain.

Kilmersdon ✤

Nestling in the foothills of the Mendips, Kilmersdon appeared in Domesday Book as Chenemersdone, meaning 'merestone' or 'boundary stone'.

It is largely an estate village owned partly by Lord Hylton of Ammerdown and partly by a charitable housing association. It was never solely agricultural. There was coal mining in Somerset in the Middle Ages, and Kilmersdon was always a community not just of peasants but of miners. The industry is dead now. Kilmersdon Colliery was the last to be closed almost twenty years ago and the population has declined from eight hundred at the turn of the century to little more than half that today.

The village has recently been designated a Conservation Area and of all its ancient buildings the parish church of St Peter and St Paul is its focal point and its pride. It has in fact had more than one restoration and was largely rebuilt in the 15th century by the Botreau family, perhaps in thanksgiving for deliverance from the Black Death which was extremely virulent in the area and wiped out several of the surrounding villages.

The tower rises a hundred feet above the West door, dominating the village square. Although many of the niches are empty there are still about fifty carved figures round the outside of the church. Most of the buildings, like the church itself, are of limestone. The old rectory is the most ancient, parts of it 14th century. The old school house and the manor house are mainly Elizabethan, and the Jolliffe Arms, built in the Regency style around 1830, is an impressive structure.

Kilmersdon boasts one famous legend. A hill winds up from the village to the school and at the top is a well which was the scene of Jack and Jill's disastrous accident. They were not children. They were man and wife, and the local name of Gilson is said to derive from 'Jill's son', a child of this pair. And the cottage where they landed up after their fall is still called Tumbler's Bottom.

In Victorian times there was a Friendly Society known as The Shepherds, and their Club Day was the greatest event in the village calendar. Both The Shepherds and the Club Day have long since gone, but they have worthy successors. Kilmersdon now has a Village Day, held on Spring Bank Holiday Monday each year.

Despite the demise of the coal industry, the mechanisation of agriculture and almost non-existent public transport, the village is a going concern. Homes are let by the Housing Association to couples with children so that the V.A. Church of England school is flourishing. There is a flourishing herb farm, and embryo rural industries are starting to appear.

Kingsbury Episcopi

Kingsbury Episcopi sounds very grand – King's Manor and Bishop's House. In the Domesday Book it was called Kingesberia. The actual parish of Kingsbury Episcopi covers a large area and takes in several small hamlets – East Lambrook, Mid Lambrook, West Lambrook, Stembridge, Burrow and Thorney, all delightful little places in their separate ways. The village of Kingsbury Episcopi itself has all the charm of bygone years whilst coping with modern day progress. There is an abundance of pretty cottages and gracious houses some dating far back in history. Modern architecture has to be part of today but it has managed to merge with the old world charm.

The village is situated on the edge of the moors or wetlands, a wonderful expanse of winding droves, withy beds and patchwork fields, a conservationist's dream in plant and wildlife. On the opposite side of the village is the river Parrett which meanders through green pastures to Thorney and beyond. Almost on the banks of the Parrett is the church of St Martin, a noble stone structure particularly worth photographing and must be seen by night, floodlit.

At the heart of the village is the small green on which stands the round house which is an ancient lock up.

The lock-up on the village green at Kingsbury Episcopi

97

The village must have been a hive of activity at the turn of the century. There was a blacksmith, butcher, baker, draper, saddler, post office, grocery and sweet shops, three public houses, chapel and church. All is not lost, however, there is still the chapel and the church, one public house and two shops, one incorporating the post office. There is even a small glove factory to provide employment for the ladies. The village school is situated in the hamlet of Stembridge, which is the centre of the parish.

Kingsdon 🌿

Kingsdon is on a hill of about 300 feet, affording excellent views over the flat Somerset countryside. The population is 250.

The village is part of an estate, now owned by the Neale family, who no longer live locally. However only the five farms and a few cottages remain in the estate, all the other dwellings are now privately owned. Through the active Parish Council, the Planning Committee endeavours to maintain the character of the village when houses are built, and much local lias and Hamstone is used. Many good conversions have been completed, but little thatch remains.

Originally called Kingsdon Cary, first mention of it was made in the 12th century, which is when All Saints' church was built. The 70 foot tower is a feature, and dominates the village, as is the effigy of a Knight in Hamstone of the 13th century.

Sporting and social life is well catered for with active cricket and badminton clubs, along with the Seniors' club, and a very busy WI. Kingsdon Inn is a popular meeting place. The Hunt occasionally starts off in the village, and regular shoots take place in season in Kingsdon Woods.

Primary and Junior age levels are covered at the flourishing village school. The public bus service to Yeovil and Taunton is constantly being reduced and more and more residents, without their own transport, have to depend on the village shop and post office.

The original Kingsdon manor house has been taken over and converted by the Avon Council, for children needing special attention. Many residents are employed there, as are many at Yeovilton Air Base. Otherwise, residents work at the various nearby towns, although there are a goodly number of retired people settled in the area.

The nearby Lytes Cary, now National Trust property, is a typical Somerset stone-built manor house, with its own chapel from the 15th century.

Kingston St Mary 🌿

The village of Kingston (St Mary, its full title, was only adopted some thirty years ago for postal convenience) can be found at the foot of the Quantock Hills.

The name is derived from the 13th century church of St Mary which has been called the 'gem of the Quantock group' because of its perfected Somerset tower, which also has Hunky Punks, medieval carved creatures to ward off evil.

Many of its houses and cottages are named after former residents. The oldest 16th century house is Bobbetts which was named in the 18th century after one John Bobbett. It is reputed to be haunted. The house, along with several others in the centre of the village, has now been listed as a building of outstanding and architectural interest.

Everyone has heard of the Kingston Black Apple, as it is renowned as one of the best cider apples for blending with others. During its Diamond Jubilee year in 1983 the WI planted a commemorative apple tree in the Spinney, which is a secluded area of woodland containing many British and foreign trees, and which in the spring is carpeted with snowdrops, daffodils and the rarer fritillary. It has recently been bequeathed to the Woodland Trust.

Many years ago the village was self-sufficient containing two blacksmiths, cider makers, a cordwainer, quiltmaker, tanner, soapmaker, weaver, cooper, dyers, dressmaker, tailor and many carpenters. Some skills are still retained in the village by the Church Farm Weavers, who in a converted 13th century ciderbarn, carry on weaving using local fleeces and vegetable dyes. They specialise in vestments and altar cloths.

The Old Bakery (it used to be the village post office and bakery many years ago) as well as serving coffee and cream teas is the home of the Somerset Cake Decorating Centre.

Gerald and Agnes Hooper, well known for their healing, reside at The Sanctuary with its distinctive white doves on top of the gate. People visit them from all over the country – indeed the world.

Leigh upon Mendip 🌿

With a population of about 350, Leigh stands 700 feet up in the heart of the Mendips.

St Giles church, dating back to the 15th century, is noted for its decorated tower housing six bells and a faceless clock. From the top of the tower there is a panoramic view across the countryside to the Westbury White Horse. In 1857 the village made news when the parson, one G. A. Mahon, was shot in the pulpit by one of the villagers upset by the vicar's criticism of drunkenness. Fortunately Mr Mahon was only slightly injured but his assailant was imprisoned for two years.

The old vicarage dates back to 1598 and Great House Farm nearby was built in Elizabethan times and contains some old floor tiles incorporating the letter 'E'. Either side of the church are the pilgrims' cottages, where weary travellers stayed on their way to Glastonbury and the Bell Inn, dating back to that time, was also a hostel.

In the 19th century Leigh was perhaps best known for its connection with the Fussells Iron Works at Mells. Two chimneys can still be seen which were used for steam heating wood for the handles of the then famous Fussells tools.

Litton 🌿

As far back as the days of Alfred the Great, the manor of Litton was important enough to be sold to Bishop Giso by King Alfred. It was later mentioned in the Domesday Book and referred to as the Sleepy Village.

From that time, it has been a farming area. Traces of intensive farming before 1300, when pressure of increased population forced the tilling of every possible piece of land, can still be seen on the hillside, where they were terraced, known as lychetts.

Litton owes its position as an early settlement to its plentiful supply of water, the stream running through the village. Its importance is apparent from the recording of three mills, and in the 19th century when Bristol Waterworks Company capped the local springs at Watery Combe and piped water to Bristol, they created a reservoir to ensure enough flow of water for the local millers. Today the mills have gone, the population has been halved, but the water remains to add to the charm of this small village.

The church is very important, the earliest recording being 1176 although the present building dates mainly from the late 14th century and has many interesting features, inside and out. Lovely old cottages and an ancient pub are further attractions to visitors.

Long Sutton 🙂

The village of Long Sutton has a village green with a lime tree at each corner and a chestnut tree in the centre. The Devonshire Arms Hotel is at one end of the green and at the other the school and Holy Trinity church which is noted for its lovely wooden pulpit, said to be the oldest in England.

The village is made up of two hamlets – Knole at one end and Upton at the other. Knole is famous for its waterwheel, dating back to the 11th century, as well as two very old farmhouses. The old barns are now converted into dwelling houses. The main line railway runs under the bridge at Upton and at one time certain trains stopped at Long Sutton and Pitney Halt as it was called. It was a common sight on market days to see the drovers driving a herd of cattle or a flock of sheep to various farms, but regretfully the station was closed some years ago and animals are hauled around in cattle lorries.

The Quaker Meeting House was built in Queen Anne style and finished in 1717. It is very well preserved to this day and is still used for worship by the Quakers. There is a famous mounting block outside used in olden days to mount and dismount their horses when they came to worship, worshippers coming from as far away as Street, nearly seven miles away.

Opposite the Quaker Meeting House, known as Quakers' Corner are two cottages, once thatched. In one of these cottages it is said that Mrs Palmer of Huntley and Palmer fame made her first biscuits and cakes to help provide for her family. Some of the grave stones mark the resting-place of the Palmer family in the grounds of the Friends' Meeting House.

Punkie Night originated many years ago and was started by farm labourers to light their way home after work. It is now the 'children's night' and held on the nearest night to Halloween. The children carry their 'punkies' made from either mangolds, turnips or marrows, which are hollowed out and faces or animals carved on them and lit with a candle inside.

Lydeard St Lawrence 🙂

Lydeard St Lawrence lies away from the main road from Taunton to Minehead, set between the Quantock Hills and the Brendon Hills. The

Celtic word 'Lydeard' signifies 'gateway' or 'pass' and was formerly Lidiard.

Dominating the village street is the large sandstone church standing on the steep rise of the hill, the oldest part being the decorated chancel. The Tudor bench ends are richly carved and the capitals of the arcade show some interesting carving, one picturing a fox seizing a goose. Up to about 1858 there was a string band to lead the music for church services. The band sat in the gallery at the west end of the church.

Opposite the church is the village County Primary School with its attractive neo-Tudor chimneys and which celebrated its centenary in 1976. North of the school and also opposite the church, is the manor house, once the home of the Hancock family, an important land-owning family in the parish in earlier times.

This is a farming community. Tractors and trailers are frequently seen moving up and down the village street and there is one farm right in the middle of the village. Under the street and through that farmland flows a stream fed by a spring which never fails. This spring gushes, fresh and cold through an opening in an old sandstone wall, and reputedly posses-ses medicinal properties.

Lydeard St Lawrence is a friendly village, a caring village – and nowhere is this neighbourliness shown more clearly than in the village post office, the village shop and the village bakery. Within living memory, there was also a butcher's shop in the village, a forge and a second grocer's shop and up to this present time residents take their Christmas and special dinners along to the bakery to be cooked, a long held custom.

Lympsham

The first references to the village of Lympsham come in the middle of the 12th century. At that time it was called Lymplesham and was owned by the Abbots of Glastonbury. It is, however, in more recent times that the village had a period which seems to make it quite unique.

For 103 years, apart from a short gap of seven years, from 1809 to 1912 the incumbents of St Christopher's church were three generations of one family. This began when, on 15th July 1809, Joseph Adam Stephenson was appointed Rector. His great concern was education and he built a school room for the village in 1820, in the eastern corner of the churchyard.

On 8th March 1844 his son Joseph Henry was appointed. He was to

102

remain as Rector for 57 years until he died in 1901. During these years he was a much loved and respected minister.

In the middle of the 19th century the average housing for farm workers was poor in the extreme, countryside slums in fact. The Rector set about improving matters in 1863, and over the next 30 years or so, built some 17 houses, all in stone in the Gothic style, very tall chimneys and, on the front of each, set in the stonework, an Old English 'S'. These houses, all now privately owned, give Lympsham today its own particular appearance. In addition, in 1873, he built the school and village hall, called the Manor Hall – both used to this day.

Edmond Herbert Stephenson was the youngest son of Joseph Henry, born in 1859. He was appointed to Lympsham church in June 1901, after serving as vicar of Assington, Suffolk. He was not nearly so wealthy as his father and grandfather before him. The manor house, which had served as rectory for so many years, was now occupied by his elder brother. Edmond Herbert, the last of the Stephenson Rectors, left Lympsham in 1912 to emigrate to Canada.

One hundred years of love and care had been given to the village of Lympsham by these three generations of ministers. They had wrought great improvements to church and village and the appearance of both, even to this day, is due in great measure to the Stephenson family.

Mark 🦩

Mark is a farming community, keeping mixed breeds of sheep, Friesian dairy cows and beef cattle. The pastures are on moorland clay, so are rather wet in winter, especially for the sheep.

The older houses and cottages have been carefully brought up-to-date, and about half the houses here have been built in the last 30 years. This has brought in more people, making a livelier and less restrained populace!!

The village is to be found 4 miles along the B3139 country road, which runs between Highbridge and Wells, in the north of Somerset. The Mendip Hills are to the north, and the lights on the Polden Hills are visible to the south, across Mark and Burtle Moors.

The name Mark has been written several ways through the ages. March meaning 'a marsh' and Mercon and mainly Merk 'a boundary'. It would seem to be on the edge of the flooded marsh and at the end of the higher ridge running through Mark, Blackford, Wedmore, Panborough and Wells: each of which were islets!

On the very large and rather beautiful Village Map of 1886, the cider orchards are much in evidence. Every farm had a cider-house and press. There are still several cider-makers locally, who have been in the business many years.

There is new life now at Mark House, one of the grandest Georgian houses, in the guise of a private school for boys. There are over 30 young people in residence. The house is probably the latest building on this site, upon the higher ridge, near Uplands.

The large and benignly imposing church is on the perfect village site, overlooking the square and it is a place where most of the village gets together.

The Pack Horse inn was important to the wool merchants of the Mendip Hills who transported their wool, etc, through Mark on their way to the ports of Highbridge and of the Bristol Channel. They stopped at the inn to change horses, and pick up the wool from sheep grazing on these lowlands.

A recent feature noticeable above the roofs is the interesting variety of weather vanes – a tractor, black and white cow, a curly tailed pig, an Alsatian's head, cockerel and a running fox.

Marston Bigot

The village of Marston Bigot is situated two miles south of Frome, just off the A361 Frome to Shepton Mallet road. The panoramic views from the A361 across the valley to Cley Hill and the Longleat estate in Wiltshire show why the area has been designated 'of outstanding natural landscape value'.

Originally Marston Bigot was a manorial estate, which at the time of the Norman Conquest was called Mersilone. It later became Marston, which is old English for marsh, the surrounding area being marshland. In the reign of Henry III, the Lord of the Manor, Bigod or Bigot added his name. The Bigots were a branch of the Earl of Norfolk's family.

In the 18th and 19th century, the Earl of Cork and Orrery owned the estate. A feudal system existed: the estate farms, which were all dairy farms, were either worked by tenants or by employees for the Lord of the Manor.

The estate church, St Leonard's, was built in the Norman style and is approached from Marston House on a yew lined path. The Duke of Somerset was and still is patron of St Leonard's and all other churches in the district. The most well-known incumbents of St Leonard's church were Rector Boyle and his wife Eleanor. A well which was built outside the local school for the use of the poor by Mr Boyle was named Eleanor's Well. Now the school has been converted for residential use, but Eleanor's Well remains.

The remainder of the estate cottages and farms have been sold piecemeal. Cottages have been renovated and are now used for retirement or by commuters to surrounding towns. The farms are now privately owned, and are mostly still dairy farms, although since the advent of the European Economic Council's milk quota, some sheep farming and a little cereal growing has begun.

Martock

Martock is a large village, just off the A303 between the old Roman towns of Ilchester and Ilminster. To the north is Stapleton and Coat and to the south Hurst and Bower Hinton, hamlets now forming part of Martock. Throughout the parish there are a number of lovely old houses built of the honey coloured Hamstone which was quarried on nearby Hamdon Hill. Many of the houses have interesting features such as delicate ironwork to the windows, gables peculiar to the immediate area, and some are thatched. In recent times there has been development of modern estates providing homes for many people and this is continuing with more new houses being built on the site of the old abbatoir in North Street.

In the centre of Martock is the Market House which, at one time, housed the fire engine, and the fire bell can still be seen on the roof of the building. In front of the Market House is a tall column known as The Pinnicale and nearby is the 14th century manor house and the old coaching inn, The White Hart Hotel. The parish church of All Saints is justly famous for its magnificent carved roof and lofty nave. To the west of the church is The Moat House, now a new house on the old site and alas there is no moat but it was one of the few in Somerset. The Treasurer's House, opposite the church, is a 13th–15th century house (now owned by The National Trust) and was the home of the Treasurer of Wells Cathedral.

Martock is a lively community with more than 50 organisations catering for all interests and all age groups. The Carnival has been revived and a keen band of villagers work hard throughout the year raising money to finance Carnival Day.

On the small industrial estates there are a number of factories and units providing work for local people and these include glovemaking, tentmaking, a timber yard, printing, engineering plus many more new businesses now setting up on the site of the former Harry Hebditch factory where portable timber buildings were made.

For the gardeners of the area we even have our own 'Martock Bean' – rather rare but still grown in some secret places.

Meare & Westhay 🌿

The parish of Meare includes the village of Westhay and the hamlets of Stileway and Oxenpill. Meare was previously an island called 'Feramere' and Westhay was known as 'Westeie' (the 'eie' meaning island). Being part of the Somerset Wetlands, it is known for its peat, which has been dug here for at least the last 2000 years.

Meare is steeped in history both above and below the ground. It is famous as the site of a former primitive lake village and there have been many interesting finds by the peat diggers over the years. A prehistoric footpath dating from 4000 BC made to allow early fishermen and hunters to cross the areas of reed and marshlands and a dug out boat are among the finds.

The village church is mainly 14th century and has a medieval stone pulpit and the south door is decorated with medieval wrought iron work. Next door to the church is the old manor house which was built as a retreat for the Abbots of Glastonbury. Parts date back to 1340. Nearby is the Fish House where the catch taken from the Abbot's fishpool was salted and stored for the use of the monks at Glastonbury in the 14th century. The Fish House is supposed to have a secret underground tunnel linking up with Glastonbury Abbey, but this has never been proved.

From their very small beginnings the villages have become much larger over the last 30 years, providing homes for people working in nearby towns. Although the peat industry and farming have been the main forms of employment in the villages, in recent years small businesses have been started including engineering and sheepskin products.

The village school has always been a meeting place for old and new alike and today the school is still thriving with over 100 primary school children, who when they reach the age of 11 go to the comprehensive at Glastonbury.

Mells

Mells is Jack Horner's Plum! Jack Horner worked in the office of Thomas Cromwell when the monasteries were being broken up, and 'acquired' Mells at this time and built himself a Tudor mansion.

The church has a wonderful spire, and slender, tapering pinnacles, and inside there are many surprises, a carved peacock by Burne-Jones, an art-nouveau window, and a bronze equestrian statue by Sir Alfred Munnings! Mells is in quarrying country, on the edge of a coal-field, and surrounded by rich lands. It had iron-works too, but its main industry was cloth-making. It had its own woad plantation for dying, and the fullers earth for the tucking mills was brought from the country round Wellow and English Combe.

Merridge

Merridge is just a few houses strung along two roads. In the last 30 years a public house, small shop and sub-post office have closed, as more families own cars and can more easily reach the towns of Taunton and Bridgwater.

At one time the local children could attend the Aisholt & Merridge School. This was closed at the beginning of the Second World War, when it was used as a store. In 1951 this stone-built building was purchased from the Church Authorities, the owners, by subscription by the residents. Since then it has been used as a village hall.

Merriott

Merriott is a large village in South Somerset, close to the Devon and Dorset borders. It derives its name from the Anglo-Saxon Maergeat, meaning 'boundary gate'. In 1066 the manor of Merriott belonged to Eadnoth, Master of the King's Horse and Commander of the Men of Somerset, whose family took the name de Meriet.

John de Meriet built a church near his manor house and in 1276 his infant son was baptized there. The lower part of the present church and a stone crucifix date back to the 13th century. No trace of the manor house remains.

The manor lands were split up in the middle 1800s. Some of the villagers bought a couple of acres and started market gardening. The soil in the village is very fertile. Nurseries were mentioned in 1375. By the 19th century there were several nurseries in the village. In 1852 John Scott purchased the largest of them. In his handbook and catalogue called the Orchardist (you can see a copy in the Somerset Records Office), he claimed he had ransacked the nurseries of Europe to find over 1000 varieties of fruit trees in the Merriott nurseries. Scott's Nurseries and garden centre are still flourishing today and are widely known.

Another source of work at that time was making rope and sailcloth at Tail Mill. Using their own breed of sturdy fast horses called Merriott half-breeds, they would haul the flax to the factory, or take the finished cloth to the ships and boats at the coast and then return with loads of fish which they sold in the village when they got home.

But where are our farmers and market gardeners now? Only two or three remain, and much of that fertile soil has been used for modern houses and estates. Some of our older houses date back to the 1600s, and are built of Hamstone, but they are mainly family homes. Many of the farmhouses have been restored and tidied up.

The little shops which used to sell a few groceries and household items have gone, but new ones have sprung up that cater for most needs. The two pubs serve meals and the streets are as well lit as any towns. Most of the workers find employment at Westlands and the factories in the area. The village school has a good supply of pupils for the juniors, and a middle and senior school are within easy reach.

Middlezoy

The name Middlezoy derives from Sowey, a fertile island. Middlezoy and Chedzoy were fertile islands in the days before the reclamation of the Somerset Levels, which was begun in the 13th century by the great ecclesiastical land-owners, and they were the centres for the drainage schemes, which were not to be completed for centuries. During Monmouth's Rebellion in 1685 the king's soldiers camped in the church, and one of them is buried there.

Milborne Port 🐚

Milborne Port has some strange contradictions. Firstly it is not a port on the coast, for port is an old Saxon word for town or market and it is some 30 miles from the Dorset coast. Milborne is easier to understand and literally translated means 'Mill on the stream'. There were mills here, glove and leather mills – in fact in years gone by an enormous amount of leather work was done in the home and taken to markets in Yeovil.

The second contradiction is the road sign pointing to the new village hall built only a few years ago – strangely situated for this sign is opposite the old town hall! And the third contradiction? Milborne Port is geographically in Somerset but its postal address is Sherborne, Dorset!

The 18th century town hall stands on the corner of South Street and High Street, a square, mellowed, stone building. Once it was open with archways and under these archways a market was held each week.

Milborne Port was important in days gone by, having associations with Saxon Kings. The oldest doorway to be seen is of Norman design with zig zag carving – the doorway of the Guild Hall is in the High Street. Milborne Port even sent representatives to Parliament until the 1830s. Since those days its importance has declined.

The old school is the lovely building with a clock tower at the Gainsborough corner, but is now a Recording Studio. The new school in North Street is a busy primary school of some 200 pupils.

Bread is baked by old farmhouse methods at Tom Coombs, the bakehouse in the centre of the village – an old family business that has been baking bread for 4 generations.

The A30 cuts the village in half, a narrow busy stretch of road re-named as the High Street as it passes through the village and most of the shops. Traffic congestion builds up on a Saturday morning and throughout the summer.

The parish church has a majestic square tower and inside and outside one can see Norman arches. It is said it is probably the oldest church in Somerset. The Methodist church is large by village standards, built in the 19th century and has the most beautiful rose window. By contrast the United Reformed Church is small, Victorian and hidden away down Chapel Lane.

Milverton 🌿

Milverton is an ancient village of some 1300 people, off the A361 between Taunton and Wiveliscombe. It is set amidst scenes of crops and pastures in the Vale of Taunton Deane, its rich red earth and sandy loam, and sheltered dampness, making it rich agricultural country. It was once a woollen centre and there are many attractive Georgian houses dating from the time of greatest prosperity.

The parish church is high on the hill, with a tall red tower but no steeple. It is noted for its old carved bench-ends.

There has been a school here since the days of the Dame School, when payment had to be made. A bequest by Mary Lambe encouraged education and today's Victorian school is a county primary – with a new school planned.

There is a revival of interest in old customs and community action. Milverton had a market at the time of the Norman Conquest, and a market day is now held monthly. A flower show, in spring and autumn, encourages contributions from young and old alike. The Court Leet has been revived as has the ancient custom of Beating the Bounds. Footpaths receive attention so that they can be carefully defined. The annual village fete grows ever more popular and more profitable.

A famous resident in the 1800s was Thomas Young. He had a great interest in Egyptology and studied hieroglyphics, leading to his being able to help decipher the famous Rosetta Stone.

In more recent years the shadow of the developer has fallen to some extent over Milverton, to a plea from those who live there:

> 'No stick-in-mud is Milverton as shown in days now past.
> It can with vision, courage, wit adapt, but not TOO FAST.'

Misterton 🌿

As with other villages, Misterton has changed a lot over the years and is still changing.

Along Church Lane is The Old Coach-House which at one time must have been fairly humble servants' quarters, serving the manor house – an impressive Georgian building with a grand drive sweeping up to it but now split into three quite large dwellings. The original manor house was not here but at Old Court.

110

Middle Street is the main road through the village. Here is The Thatched Farm House, its thatch a beautiful reminder of the past but its front a sad reminder of the present. For it has had to be strengthened to withstand the impact of cars which so often take the corner too quickly and crash into it. This village street was meant for horses and carts not modern traffic. Next door stand Estate House and Estate Cottage back to back like sulking lovers. They were built in 1879 as one building to serve as the estate office for the Portman estate. In Estate House one can still see where tenants came to pay their rent and legend has it that Lord Portman could ride from Somerset to Portman Square in London without ever leaving his own property.

In 1988 The White Swan and The Globe are the only pubs in Misterton, but it is not many years since there were some six or seven and in Silver Street, past three lovely 17th century houses, are the sites of two former hostelries.

At the turn of the century not only were there more pubs in Misterton but also several shops and businesses as compared with the one post office stores now. These included a blacksmith, a wheelwright, a rope and net maker, a bakery and baker's shop, a butcher and most important Mrs Higgens' grocery shop. Here you could have seen whole cheeses on the counter and boys sent to fetch the groceries waited until Mrs Higgens left the counter to steal a few crumbs of cheese. Mrs Higgens was onto them however, and boys soon found that the 'cheese crumbs' were in fact soap!

Montacute ✌

The Domesday book records that 'The Count himself holds Bishopston in Lordship'; the Count being Robert of Mortain (in Normandy), half-brother of William the Conqueror. The name of Bishopston is still in use – its wide street being very much a feature of the village, leading to the parish church of St Catherine.

Robert's son, William, founded a Cluniac Priory in honour of St Peter and St Paul in 1102, which was later granted a charter by the King enabling the monks to operate a market. This took place in the open area known as the Borough. The Abbey was lost at the time of the Dissolution but happily the gatehouse, fishpond and dovecote remain.

Montacute is predominantly built of Hamstone – the mellow golden stone quarried to this day on nearby Ham Hill, which has provided jobs

The village of Montacute

for many stonemasons over the years. Hamstone was used in the construction of the magnificent Montacute House, built by the Phelips family and now owned by the National Trust.

The pointed hill (in Latin Mons Acutus) to the west of the village, gives Montacute its name. Since 1760 it has been topped by a tower, also built by the Phelips family – giving rise to tales of secret passages to the House. The tower affords wonderful views over much of the Somerset countryside and has recently been restored – making the climb to the top of St Michael's Hill well worth the effort although the largest rookery in Somerset which was to be found here early in this century has long since 'taken wing'.

There is a medical foundation in Melbourne investigating heart disease, which bears the name of a Montacute family. It was a member of this family too who built the unique church clock over 300 years ago. A descendant of the maker made the daily journey to the church to wind the clock for 65 years, retiring in 1984. The clock has now been restored and its chimes once again ring out – marking the passage of time as it adds yet more chapters to the history of Montacute.

Moorland

There are no surprises in the derivation of Moorland's name. Midway between Huntworth and Burrowbridge, it perches beside the river Parrett, surrounded by the moors, the famous Wetlands which sheltered King Alfred from the Danes. Only a few feet above sea-level, a watery waste in winters past, it is a mystery how it ever developed as a village. The road along which it straggles was, and still is, its only link with other villages. A lane links the village with its hamlet, Fordgate, and ends at the Bridgwater–Taunton canal. A row of old, small cottages, is sandwiched between the canal, opened in 1827, and the railway, built in 1846. They once included a small chapel and an inn. Attractively decorated and modernised, they reflect the tenacity of the people of the moors.

Several droves lead from the village on to the moors. In the past, the roads were almost impassable in winter. The droves still are. Yet, Moorland is mentioned as early as 1279 as being within the bounds of Petherton Forest. In 1685 villagers must have trembled in their beds, as the Battle of Sedgemoor thundered a mile away across the river.

The church, young by Somerset standards, was built in 1843. In 1860 it was the centre of riots when the vicar was foolish enough to try to introduce the High Church Oxford Movement to villagers whose ancestors had been Dissenters and supporters of the rebellious Duke of Monmouth. One curate wrote that the people were rough and lawless, even semi-barbarous.

In the past many men in the village were boatmen. Now the only fishermen are found in early spring when the elvers come up the river Parrett. The great wide nets are taken from sheds and barns, and every night winking lights are seen along the banks. The thin bootlace like fish provide a tasty breakfast – in harder times they were the main meal. Rayballs made of worms were used to catch the more substantial parent eel.

Today the village is still ringed with farms. The cows plod daily along the droves in summer, tractors rumble along the lanes. There are several families whose ancestors have lived here for generations. Moorland is a vital community. The school, frequently threatened with closure, continues to thrive. The village hall is the pride of the residents, who literally built it themselves. The Pumping Station, like a mechanical heart, pumps the water along the rhines into the river, ensuring that flooding is minimal, and unlikely to reach the 6 feet that rose in the church in 1880 and marooned the villagers in their homes in 1929.

Moorland may lack the chocolate-box prettiness of some villages, but it has a priceless asset – every house has the sweeping moors for a garden. To walk along the droves on a summer's evening, to see nothing but the great arc of the sky above, and the lush green meadows around, to savour the silence and be aware of the timelessness of the surroundings, makes living in Moorland worthwhile.

Mudford 🌿

Mudford, together with the nearby villages of Marston Magna and West Camel, is situated in a low-lying area just north of Yeovil. It once contained seven hamlets, of which two have completely disappeared (Nether Adber and Mudford Terry) and three are much shrunken (Hinton, West Mudford and Up Mudford). In 1633, Thomas Gerrard, of nearby Trent, wrote that 'the Huntley family flourished at Nether Adber, even until our grandfathers' days, when all of a sudden it sunk'. The lovely parish church of St Mary, however, still remains.

Marston Magna has a brook running through the village that turned a mill until the Second World War, and once served the moat of a long vanished manor house, whereas West Camel boasts a great barn, nearly as old as the church, and a pigeon-house with over 600 niches.

Nether Stowey 🌿

Nether Stowey lies at the foot of the Quantock Hills overlooking the lowlands of the Severn estuary. Dominated by the Mount, the site of Stowey Castle which was destroyed in the Wars of the Roses, it is an attractive village of mixed architectural styles with several listed buildings. Once a market town of some 600 people it seems always to have been a thriving community.

Among the famous names connected with Stowey – the word probably means 'paved road' – that of Samuel Taylor Coleridge springs first to mind. Much of his best known poetry was written whilst he was resident in the cottage in Lime Street which today is open to the public and administered by the National Trust.

Traces of cobbles remain in many places and the Toll House reminds us that the village was on a coach route. It is said that there were 13 inns at that time! The centre of the village is still known as the Cross although the cross-surmounted yarn market which gave it that name has long since disappeared.

Villagers enjoy 'Commoners Rights' though few today avail themselves of the privileges. Only farmers now graze their sheep on the hills. Wortleberries are still picked but a generation or two ago whole families would spend days picking on the hills, selling the berries for 1½d or 2d per quart.

Today, Nether Stowey is still a bustling village and has been much enlarged in recent years. The tower is the oldest part of the well-cared-for church most of which was rebuilt in the middle of the last century. With Stowey Court it is, unfortunately, cut off from the village by a very necessary by-pass. The Court is said to contain stones from the castle in its walls and still possesses its original trout ponds. Its fine gazebo is visible from the road. Church, village hall, three pubs, several shops, stable, garage and a modern school cater for the varying needs of the village.

Over Stowey, by contrast to its sister village, is a tranquil place and, with its surrounding hamlets, is also steeped in history. The church is chiefly remarkable for its recently-restored Burne-Jones window and the churchyard in spring is a sight to behold – a carpet of wild daffodils, primroses and celandines.

North Cadbury 🌿

North Cadbury is situated half a mile from the A303 in the heart of countryside that abounds with legend and history, set among fields and orchards of cider apple trees. The parish is large and incorporates North Cadbury, Woolston and Galhampton making it one of the biggest in the area. Cadeberia, together with Woolston, was mentioned in the Domesday Book and means fortified hill. The village lies north of Cadbury Camp – Arthur's Camelot.

The ancient Catash Hundred Courts, Danish in origin, were held locally and the local inn is named after this historic fact. The Catash Inn

Cottages at North Cadbury

continues to provide refreshment, food and social contact for their customers.

The fine Elizabethan manor house now known as The Court was built in 1581 by Sir Francis Hastings, and 99% of the village remained with one owner until 1877. The parish church dedicated to St Michael the Archangel owes its beginnings to Lady Elizabeth Botreaux and was founded as a Collegiate Church in 1417. The oak pews are famous dated 1538 with carved ends depicting scenes of village life, village characters and a Tudor mouse trap (cat with mouse). Local stone was used for many of the cottages and some are still thatched making a picturesque feature. The Hall Cottage is a cruck frame building, 15th century in origin with 16th century renovations.

The village had an active watermill and the waterfall still runs to delight young and old alike. Numerous shops supplied a wide selection of goods but the 20th century has made many changes and only the post office with general store remains.

Woolston is a hamlet and was mainly smallholdings, long since gone and now merged into larger farms. It is a pleasant place with cottages and a busy market garden famous for soft fruit fields and other fresh produce.

Galhampton, described as a 'cottagers village' had several large farms but no squire. There is a manor house with peacocks and hens walking in the gardens. During the last 20 years a vast number of dwelling houses have been built, changing the appearance of the village. The small church, largely Victorian, is home for the Galhampton joint church, ie United Reformed and Church of England.

Galhampton has two agricultural engineering businesses and an agricultural contractor that makes employment in this rural area. The local Inn is named The Harvester reflecting this trade. Mr John Robinson, the internationally famous sculptor, lives and works at Galhampton. One of his set pieces the 'Rise and fall of man' is displayed in the churchyard at North Cadbury.

North Cheriton 🐟

North Cheriton lies on the edge of the Blackmoor Vale in South Somerset.

The name of the village is from the Saxon words meaning 'the enclosure or village with a church' – so clearly there was a church on or near the site of the present one before the Norman Conquest. The building has a fine perpendicular west tower and was remodelled (apart from the tower) in 1878, at which period the chancel and organ chamber were erected. The chancel is markedly 'offset' from the nave, and this is clearly deliberate, but the reason is uncertain. The churchyard, now closed, contains the stump of a stone cross which is reputed to be Saxon.

The stocks outside the church gate date from the 16th century, with a roof added quite recently to protect them. Opposite lies the war memorial, erected by the parishoners in 1921, on land which formed part of a local charity, the Gale Trust. The impressive manor house by the church is 19th century and is built of local stone. The manor itself was held by Ernni, a Saxon, in 1066 and there is a full description of it in the Domesday Book as 'Cireton'.

The village pump, almost opposite the village hall, is an interesting relic of the early 19th century. It is of cast iron and was made by Portnell of Wincanton. The old post office is probably over 300 years old, but of course it has been much altered. It is now a private house, as is the old school built in 1846. The school at North Cheriton survived longer than most small village schools, finally closing in 1977.

Parts of the Old Red Lion, privately-owned since 1958, date back to the 17th century, but it is not certain how long it has been used as an inn. It is one of the few surviving 'long houses' left in Somerset. On the outskirts of the village there is an old barn, parts of which go back to the 18th century. The high vertical wall at right angles to the road is thought to have been built in the 17th century, and tradition has it that it was used for the game of Pelota by prisoners from the Napoleonic Wars in 1805 to 1815. They apparently used to slake their thirst at the nearby Windmill Inn.

North Curry 🦢

North Curry, which probably means 'wet plain' stands on a ridge above the Somerset Levels and the Sedgemoor plains and was the first designated conservation area in Taunton Deane. The area abounds with animal and bird life; badgers, foxes, buzzards and Bewick's swans. Wintering birds come to feed in the fields that are criss-crossed by the rhines and pollarded willows. North Curry was and still is, the centre of the willow industry which is carried on by the old families using the traditional methods of their forefathers, producing beautiful hand made baskets, wattle fences and artists' charcoal. The Willow Craft Trail can be followed and all the processes can be seen from initial planting of the withies to finished product.

The river Tone, used for transporting coal and heavy loads to Ham Bridge within living memory, runs through the Levels. It is fished not only by herons, but in the spring by men and boys with nets to catch the elvers, as they have done for centuries. All these sights are enjoyed by the walkers of the village as they set out across the moors most Saturdays following the well sign-posted footpaths. From the high ground they can enjoy the beautiful distant views and rare orchids and flowers at their feet.

The imposing church of St Peter and St Paul, known as 'The Cathedral of the Moors' whose octagonal tower dominates the landscape was built in about 1300, on the site of an earlier church. Looking down from the churchyard where there is an early Saxon cross thought to have come from the site of the abbey which Alfred built at Athelney, one can easily imagine the early parishioners arriving by boat across the flooded valley. On the hill to the east the Romans are believed to have grown vines. The church contains a peal of 8 bells, an ancient chest, some charming carvings and a fascinating account of the Reeve's Feast, the origins of which are lost in the mists of antiquity.

The Reeve, head of the village, designated dealers or dolers to give out to poor tenants on Christmas Eve pork, bread, beef and money. They in turn, with the Lords of the Manor of Knapp and Slough (The Jacks,

Listed cottages in Church Road, North Curry

Masters of Ceremonies) enjoyed a feast of beef, onions, marrow bones, bread and ale followed by mince pies, decorated with an effigy of the King. Two one-pound candles were lit at the start of the feast and, until they burned away, the Jacks and their attendants had the right to sit drinking ale. The North Curry Society have recently revived the tradition of the feast.

Church Road, leading from the church into the centre of the village is beautiful. It has many listed cottages, a central green area where the annual May Fair is held, the war memorial, and the memorial to Queen Victoria known as the Pepper Pot because of its shape. Here too is the site of The Old Pound where stray cattle and horses were impounded.

North Curry is a thriving community, with the everyday needs of the 1,400 population well catered for. The village school has recently been built to replace the old school house. One of the great advantages of North Curry is that no main road runs through the village although access to Taunton and surrounding areas is relatively easy.

North Newton

Life in the village of North Newton and its surrounding hamlets of Hedging, Tuckerton, Chadmead and West Newton has always been regarded as being one of happy prosperity. It was known for many years as 'The Garden of Eden' because of its magnificent market garden produce, which is grown in soil ranging from red sand to the dark peat of the moors.

Today, the number of market garden producers has somewhat dwindled in the area although produce is still distributed to local shops and is still eagerly sought after in the markets of Bristol and Cardiff.

The plentiful supply of apples helped to make cider-making a favourite pastime in the village – many gallons of fine cider being produced and consumed! However, as orchards made way for new homes, that occupation dwindled until there are really only one or two local cider-makers left.

In the past, many local people found employment at Maunsel House which is part of an estate of great historic interest. Parts of the house date back to the 11th century. The present owners – the Slade family – took up residence in the mid 18th century. The estate has one of the smallest churches in Somerset – St Michael's church.

The Bridgwater to Taunton canal which bounds the village is being renovated and the four locks which are included in the North Newton section have all been updated. This is another tourist attraction and it is hoped to provide picnic areas and boat trips throughout the Summer Season.

The opportunity for education began well over 100 years ago with the building of a fine stone school. Nowadays the number of scholars has dwindled considerably but the school still maintains its position as the 'heart' of the village, providing education for the under 11s to a very high standard.

A short distance from the school stands St Peter's church, parts of which originate from Saxon times – indeed, it is said that King Alfred's Jewel, which now rests in the Ashmolean Museum, Oxford, was found behind this very church. A copy of the Jewel which is inscribed 'Alfred had me made' sits inside the church.

North Perrott

North Perrott is a small village in the south of the county, on the A3066, with about 200 inhabitants. It is pleasantly situated, with some old stone houses. The church is mainly 15th century, of a cruciform plan with a central tower, and has been extensively renovated.

Villagers are proud to have amongst their number Mr Bill Hoskyns, an internationally famous British fencing champion. He has taken part in four Commonwealth Games and six Olympic Games, winning an Epee Individual Silver Medal in the Olympics of 1964.

North Petherton

'Twenty villagers, nineteen smallholders, six slaves and twenty pigmen', so runs the entry for North Petherton in the Domesday Book. Nine hundred years later North Petherton with a somewhat larger population of around 4500 is still going strong. Situated between Taunton and Bridgwater, it straddles the A38 with a collection of old and new buildings, of which the Minster church of St Mary in the centre is the most interesting. With the highly decorated 15th century tower, this is probably one of the most beautiful perpendicular churches in the county, attracting many visitors.

The name North Petherton is derived from the Petherton Forest, one of the great medieval hunting forests of Somerset, which also incorporated the monastery at Athelnay founded by King Alfred. An important North Petherton connection with King Alfred is the beautiful Alfred Jewel found in 1693. Now in the Ashmolean Museum at Oxford, the jewel is inscribed 'Aelfred Mec Heht Gewyrcan', which loosely translated means 'Alfred had me made'. Possibly the handle of a book marker, a replica of the jewel is kept at North Petherton and brought out on special occasions.

In 1878 the Board School was opened for children of all ages with a roll call of around 267. Nowadays the school building houses the junior school with the infants in new buildings nearby, and the senior pupils travel to schools in Bridgwater and Taunton.

There were 5 basket manufacturers during the 1930s using the locally picked willows, woven as baskets, wicker furniture and even coffins (which not surprisingly were not very successful).

Quantock House in Fore Street which is now flats, shops and library was built on the site of the former Quantock cider factory. Opposite Quantock House is the former George Hotel, previously a coaching inn, and until recently still a public house. Although the old exterior has been retained, the interior has been converted into several private dwellings. Several other old inns are still in existence including the Walnut Tree Inn, The Swan and the Lamb Inn all situated in Fore Street.

North Wootton 🦢

In the Domesday Book North Wootton was called Utone, the landholder was Edred and the land was owned by the Glastonbury church. There were probably 75–85 people here in 1086, now there are some 250.

The village has always been a farming one. The growing of vines has also been part of its history. Many craftsmen resided in North Wootton including a smith, a stonemason, carpenters, shoemakers and of course a thatcher – most of the houses were thatched until well into the 19th century. Cider making flourished, so there was probably a resident cooper making the barrels. A cider mill was built in the early 18th century, but much cider was made on the farms.

The river Redlake runs through the village. This joins with the Whitelake and other waterways flowing into the Hartlake river and on to the Somerset Levels.

Today farming is still the predominant way of life and there is also a flourishing vineyard. The village school closed in the 1960s. The old schoolhouse is now a private residence, as is the old cider mill, the chapel and the millhouse to name but a few. Many villagers work outside of the village or have retired here. There is no mains drainage so there has not been too much building expansion. Manor Farm, once *the* pub has been superseded by The Crossways Inn, a very popular meeting place.

The village hall, next to the church, is the meeting place for all local events. The church has always had a strong following. It boasts a Norman font. The church's rector presides over four parishes, North Wootton being one, plus Dinder & Dulcote, Croscombe and Pilton. The church is lovingly looked after by the parishioners.

For most of this century there has been a village store, but sadly it closed a few years ago leaving a large space in the everyday life of the village as it was a popular meeting place. However, a resident has converted part of her house into a post office so villagers can buy stamps and collect their pensions.

North Wootton has remained a quiet 'oasis' away from the rush of nearby Wells, Glastonbury and Shepton Mallet. It has moved with the times in some ways but the 'old days' are still recounted with great fondness.

Norton Fitzwarren

Norton Fitzwarren – a strange name, but it is said that it was formerly called Nurton or Nortone, which means North of the Tone. The Fitzwarren is derived from the name of the family who at one time lived at the manor.

The church is of great interest – especially the screen. Records show that the church was either restored or rebuilt in 1841 principally by the exertions of the Rev J P Hewett, and the chancel was also rebuilt in 1866. The churchyard contains headstones for the Royal Burials of the King and Queen of the Gypsies.

At one time the principal trade was the brewery where large quantities of malt liquor were made and sent to distant places. The village also had its own bakery and bread was delivered daily around the neighbouring villages. Things have changed and cider making is now the occupation of many workers. From a very small beginning the factory has grown and covers a large area of the village. Fleets of lorries are to be seen taking the cider around the country.

At one time many thatched houses were in the village but sadly some were destroyed by fire and others had to be pulled down. Like many other places the village has grown in size, fields have disappeared and housing estates sprung up. The latest change to the village has been the building of a new school, away from the old one which was on a dangerous corner.

A Nature Trail has been mapped out called the 'Hill Fort'. There is a local legend that before the Norman times a red dragon lived on the hill. A carving of the dragon can be seen on the screen in the village church. There was an old saying which read:

> When Taunton was a furzy down
> Norton was a Market Town

If that is correct, times have greatly changed.

Norton St Philip 🐉

The village of Norton St Philip stands on a busy cross-roads. In the past, horse-drawn coal carts from Radstock were driven through Norton on their way to Trowbridge, whilst travellers from the West Country passed through on their way to take the waters at Bath.

In the 13th century the manor of Phillips Norton, as it was then called, had formed part of the estates of the Carthusian Priory of Hinton Charterhouse. The home of the monks' bailiff at Norton is now a residential home for the elderly, whilst the old dovecote nearby is still intact, with nesting holes for over eight hundred pigeons.

The monks built a huge barn in the village, which was later converted by them into a hostelry, called the George Inn. This building dominates the crossroads today, and has massive stone walls, and a half-timbered second floor storey, built around a medieval wool hall.

The two medieval fairs granted to the monks were held at Fairfield, and on the flat ground outside the George, known as the Plain. Older villagers can still recall the fairs held on the latter site at the turn of this century, when people danced in the road, an old lady sold 'fairings', and a fiddler from Trowbridge brought a captive bear to perform for the assembled company.

The old pagan ceremony of crowning the May Queen, followed by maypole dancing, falls on the patronal feast day of the parish church of St Philip and St James. The ceremony was incorporated into the church

124

calendar of village events, and until 1980 the school children still carried out the ceremonies, walking in procession through the village streets.

In 1685, the shadow of war fell upon the village, when the Protestant Duke of Monmouth fought his only successful skirmish here, in a bid to wrest the throne from his Roman Catholic uncle, James II. The Duke was billeted at the George Inn. There, a traitor, eager to gain the price on Monmouth's head, took a pot shot at him through a window and missed. Whereupon, Monmouth is said to have laughingly remarked: 'my man, you've missed your mark, and lost your thousand pounds'. Some families living in the village today can trace their ancestry back to the twelve men hanged as rebels here after Monmouth's Rebellion failed.

The parish church is stone built and stone tiled, with a typical Somerset tower, 70 feet high. Much restored in the 19th century by Sir Gilbert Scott, it retains several good memorials. There is a tablet which records several generations of the Rundell family, who were Somerset jewellers and clockmakers. A legacy from the last of the family was used to build and endow the village school, which is still a thriving local amenity.

The present village has retained all the vitality of former years, with a church, school, shop, post office, and two, (not six), pubs as focal points of the community. The field where the twang of the bow was heard, as medieval archers practised at the butts, now rings to the crack of the willow on summer evenings as the cricket team play on the village's own recreation field of Church Mead.

Norton-sub-Hamdon ❧

Norton-sub-Hamdon, meaning Anglo-Saxon settlement under a hill fortress, lies to the west of Hamdon Hill (Ham Hill) from which for generations the golden limestone has been quarried.

The church of St Mary The Virgin, often described as a miniature cathedral, was built by the then Lord of the Manor Henry VII in the 15th century and stands on the site of a Norman church of which the porch still remains. The tower, 96 feet high to the top of the battlements, still bears the scars of the fire caused when struck by lightning on the 29th July 1894. Many memorials and the 16th century bells were destroyed. Tower Day is commemorated each year with a service of thanksgiving partly held on the top of the tower.

As a result of the fire, pigeons from the Pigeon House in the church-yard left and never returned. The Pigeon House probably the oldest

The pigeon house at Norton-sub-Hamdon

building in the village is unique and inside there are 400 nests. It once stood outside the churchyard and was owned by the Lord of the Manor. It was restored in the 1950s with a grant from the Ministry of Works.

The origins of Norton Feast have been lost in the mists of time although it is connected with the dedication day of the church and was always celebrated around the 19th September. It lasted about a week with family gatherings, badger-baiting, cock-fighting and lots of bell-ringing.

126

Flax was grown and the industry flourished until the 1840s. The weaving of sailcloth was a cottage industry and the rattle of looms was heard in every street. Until the 1930s Norton was a village of craftsmen working in stone, wood, marble and alabaster. Masons and carpenters worked in the village, which had a high reputation well known to monument architects. Carvers from London, France and Italy came to work here. Much of their work was ecclesiastical.

Blacksmiths, bakehouses and farms are long since gone and today most employment is sought outside the village. A flourishing fruit farm and market garden does provide some jobs. The village started growing in the early 1920s when the first council houses were built and continues to grow each year.

Nunney ﹖

Founded some thirteen hundred years ago by Nunna, a Saxon chief, nestling at the foot of the Mendips between Shepton Mallet and Frome, the village of Nunney, Nouin in the Domesday Book, has seen many changes.

The most prominent feature is the castle which attracts visitors from home and abroad. Originally a peaceful manor house until the time of Cromwell, the crenallated building now has only its outer walls remaining.

A street fair takes place on the first Saturday in August, an old custom revived to celebrate the Queen's Silver Jubilee, and the village Flower Show follows in September. Some seven hundred years ago both events were held in fields at the top of the village, a great event it was too, but now those fields have been built on.

Meandering through the village is Nunney Brook. Alongside the brook stands the Market Cross, but it was not always so. The Cross's original site was the churchyard until a one time vicar had it dismantled and sold, but villagers later found the pieces and, using money from a Fair Day, had it repaired and brought back to the village.

As with all villages, Nunney had its share of public houses, but one sad day in 1969 the last of the three situated in the village was closed by the brewery. However, the villagers were not going to 'dry-out' without a fight and, for the first time in living memory, an emergency meeting of the whole parish was called. A petition with four hundred names, together with a letter, was sent off to the brewery and now you can still enjoy a pint at the George.

Straying villagers in past times often found themselves spending a night in the Guard House after an evening in a local hostelry. A key is available for anyone wishing to sample the atmosphere of the Guard House which is still in existence today, but in a far better condition, having recently been restored.

Oare ❧

Oare on Exmoor is part of the tourist trail to the Doone Valley. Set in a remote part of the moor, its church of St Mary lies in a valley just behind the rolling hills only two miles away from the sea. Visitors know it as the church where Lorna Doone was 'shot'.

Odcombe ❧

> For water, wind and air
> None to Odcombe can compare

says an old rhyme. Certainly there are many springs and old wells in the village and, until the reservoir at Sutton Bingham was built in the 1950s, Odcombe Reservoir provided the main water supply to a considerable area.

Odcombe is neither quaint nor picturesque, but the houses built of weathered Hamstone have rugged charm. The dwellings near the church and in Street Lane were mostly rebuilt in the 19th or 20th century; paradoxically the oldest house in the village is in Lower Odcombe, at the foot of the hill, which is probably the 'newer' part of the village. It is the one surviving pub, the Masons Arms, a low thatched house believed to date from the 16th century.

The village lies within a couple of miles of two large country houses, Montacute and Brympton D'Evercy, but was subservient to neither. The inhabitants tended to work on farms, as stonemasons in the quarries at Ham Hill or were employed in the twine and sailcloth industries at Coker. Many women made gloves in their own homes for the local glove factories and the gloving-machine was a standard piece of furniture in many cottage kitchens. This has given the natives of Odcombe a sturdy independence, which was reinforced by the strong nonconformist influence in the area.

At Christmas the members of Odcombe Methodist church still usher in Christmas Day as they have done for many years. Late on Christmas Eve they start out to sing carols. Their journey through the village takes most of the night, as at every house or group of houses they sing a carol and call out a Christmas greeting, so that the first experience on Christmas Day is to wake in the dark and hear their voices in the still night. Some of their carols are unique and are believed to have originated at Sherborne Abbey.

During the last twenty-five years new developments have almost doubled the population of Odcombe and brought many newcomers, some of whom have contributed a great deal to the life of the village. Most people now work in Yeovil, three miles away, but the villagers are determined to retain their one remaining shop-cum-post office and also the village primary school, which celebrated its 150th anniversary in 1981.

Odcombe was the birthplace of Thomas Coryate, born in 1579, the son of the rector of Odcombe, who introduced the table fork to England.

Old Cleeve 🌿

This tiny village, near the 12th century Cistercian Cleeve Abbey at Washford, has changed little over the years. It lies near the north coast of Somerset, reached via the A39.

One lady remembers childhood visits to her grandparents, who kept the village shop and whose family had done so for generations. Sometimes there would be charabanc parties arriving for tea on the lawn – jam in glass dishes, fresh cream from the farm at the bottom of Rectory Hill, fresh milk, buttered triangles of brown and white bread, cucumber sandwiches, homemade cakes and big pots of tea – all for 2s 6d!

Visitors would wander over to the church of St Andrew opposite to spend a few quiet minutes after tea, perhaps to read the famous epitaph to George Jones, village blacksmith:

> My sledge and hammer lie reclined
> My bellows too have lost their wind
> My fire's extinct, my forge decayed
> And in the dust my body's laid
> My coal is burnt, my irons gone
> My nails are drove, my work is done.

Othery ✍

Othery is a village mid-way between Glastonbury and Taunton on the A361 road, centrally situated in Sedgemoor. The name of the village has derived from 'Other Isle' being with Middlezoy and Weston Zoyland, the original Sowy. The village has developed over the years from a mainly farming community and since 1960 approximately 60 houses or bungalows have been built.

Othery has 12 dwellings which have been listed for their architectural qualities and many of the farmhouses have been modernised, yet retain their originality.

The number of shops and Inns have been reduced over the years, but a thriving bakery still exists, also a basket maker. The post office, inn and hotel provide a service to local and passing customers. Garages have developed from premises whose trade would have been the repair of wagons, bicycles etc. The blacksmith and wheelwright are no longer in existence, neither is the mill, which was steam powered.

The church is 13th–15th century and dedicated to St Michael, its chief treasure is part of a 15th century cope. The font is 14th century and the tower 15th century. One buttress of the central tower is pierced, but for what reason is unknown. The key for the lock of the ancient carved door is over a foot long.

Adjacent to the church is a National School Room dating from 1827. The local school was opened in 1879 with 120 pupils. Today the School premises are still in use, with some modernisation, for 41 pupils aged 4–11.

There is no street lighting in the village but some street lighting existed in the form of oil lanterns in the latter part of the last century and the earlier part of this, as posters exist advertising concerts to be held for the 'Lighting Fund' to commemorate both the Coronation of Edward VII in 1902 and George V in 1910.

The road across Greylake to the Glastonbury side of the village was built as a causeway by the monks of Glastonbury Abbey, who had their market gardens at Monkton Heathfield. Othery, being just halfway, would probably have been a victualling spot for them.

Pawlett ✤

The village of Pawlett lies on rising ground midway between the towns of Highbridge and Bridgwater, and is bounded on the west side by the river Parrett. Its Norman church marks the centre of the village, which is surrounded by lush meadows. The pews, font cover and pulpit in the church are Jacobean and very beautiful, the high altar is protected by Laudian rails – a rare feature. A wall dial on the south wall was used to show the time of the next Mass. There is also a Methodist church which was built in 1855.

Before the modern A38 bridged the river Parrett at Bridgwater, a ford between Pawlett and Combwich was used by travellers from the West Country to the North. When stage coaches ran between Bristol and the West, passengers were ferried across the river at this same point. They proceeded on their way from Combwich, the coach returning with other passengers to Bristol.

In the Domesday Book the Pawlett estate was owned by Walter de Donai. John of Gaunt, son of Edward III later owned it, and it was bequeathed by his descendants to the abbey in Bristol. On the suppression of the monasteries by Henry VIII in the mid-16th century, Pawlett was given to the Richard Cooper who became the first Earl of Shaftsbury. In 1923 the whole estate was sold in lots. It contained 88 houses, which included 8 farms, and the population was about 350. Since the Second World War this has risen to 650.

There is a village hall where various events are held, including the Friendship Club and the WI. The old inn, the Shoulder of Mutton was closed in the early part of the century. The manor house was developed as a hotel in 1949. The oldest cottage in the village is dated 1675. Panelling in one of the rooms hides a priests hole.

Fishing for salmon is carried on in withy traps which are laid in a line down the river bank. The fish come in with the tide, and are caught in the traps as it recedes.

Pilton ✤

The village was originally named Pooltown and though the spellings have varied down through the ages, the name emphasises Pilton's position as a river port in more recent times and as a West Country port in the days when the Somerset Levels were under the sea. Indeed, local legend makes a strong claim that it was to Pilton that Joseph of Arimathea sailed on his visit to our shores.

The manor of Pilton was first referred to in a charter of King Ina in AD 725 and a vineyard was originally established 'on the sunny slopes of Pilton' in 1189. The manor house itself was built by Michael of Amesbury (Abbot of Glastonbury 1235–52), though only the dovecote and cellars survive from those times. Wine making continued throughout the time the manor belonged to the Abbey of Glastonbury, but had given way to hops for beer-making by the mid 19th century. The vineyard was re-established at Pilton Manor in 1966 and is once again a recognised English wine.

Pilton, with its Great House in a lovely setting and sheltered valley, became the favourite summer residence of the abbots of Glastonbury until the Dissolution, and summer 'pilgrims' once again flock here in their thousands for their solstice Pop Festival, and to sit before their pyramid!

The largest of all the Glastonbury Abbey barns was built here in the village in the 14th century by Abbot Adam de Sodbury. It is 108 feet long and 28 feet wide and the emblems of the four evangelists are carved on the gable ends. Now in private hands and only viewable by permission of the owner, it is still very impressive despite having been struck by lightning in 1964 with the resulting loss of its thatched roof.

The abbots' influence extends into the modern life of the village by way of the Parish Rooms, which were originally the abbots' Guest House.

After the Dissolution in the 16th century it became the Poor or Church House. Behind its lovely trefoil shaped windows it shares its place in the modern community with the Working Men's Club.

The road from Glastonbury to Shepton Mallet snakes along the top edge of the valley and houses a general store, a post office and the one remaining pub. The bulk of the village, with its beautiful church and many fine 17th and 18th century houses, snuggles deep into its equable, sheltered river valley in a truly green and pleasant land.

Pitney

The name of the village was originally Pitney Lortie. The name 'Lortie' came from the original landowner, Henry de Lorti, who held the land on behalf of Henry III and paid 20 shillings a year in rent to the Crown.

'Pitney' or 'Putteney' as it was then, came from an old Saxon word 'putt' for mud or mire and 'ney' denoting a small bit of land above the wet mud!

In 1828 an archeologist, Samuel Hasell, discovered a Roman villa in the village. This was one of the most perfect ever found, in size, detail and condition, with especially beautiful mosaic figures. There are many villas round here and there must have been a large Roman settlement in the area. Some years ago a village boy put his spade down, just one spit, right on to the Roman pavement at Low Ham, now in the Taunton Museum.

The earliest Rectors of the church of St John the Baptist can be traced back to 1311. In 1641 the plague struck the village and a number of villagers were buried in their own gardens. In 1853 when the chancel was being restored a very beautiful gilt-bronze 'open-work' brooch was found and this is now in the British Museum. It is thought to date from the 11th century and is of Scandinavian origin in the Viking Urnes style. It represents a coiled snake interlaced with a ribbon-like body. It is unique and known as the 'Pitney Viking Brooch'.

The village has always been mainly agricultural, lying in a valley north of the Somerton/Langport road. A number of modern dwellings have been built in recent years and more are going up now, some for people retiring here and some for younger people working at Westlands, Yeovilton and in the nearby towns. The population is increasing and is now about 350.

Porlock 🌿

Nestling as it does at the bottom of its famous hill, the village is dominated by this well-known landmark. No trouble now to the modern car but it was not always so. There are local people who can recall in their youth sitting at the bend in the road, waiting to see if the approaching car would manage the steep gradient – and if not, offering their assistance.

As a coastal village Porlock has always enjoyed the amenities of the sea although a mile or so away from the beach. A great variety of fish, from conger eel to cod, has been caught in the bay and at one time an oyster bed lay off shore and provided a livelihood for a few families until it was dredged out at the end of the 19th century by professional fishermen from the east coast. Sea trade was always important and a flourishing

Fifteenth century Dovehay Manor, Porlock

134

trade in coal from South Wales to Porlock Weir existed up to quite recent times.

Not surprisingly the area was ripe for smuggling and the 'fair trader' had everything in his favour – easy access to the sea and an area that could not adequately be patrolled. Parcels of cloth, wine and brandy were hidden in places such as Higher Doverhay farmhouse where a false wall was discovered to have been built outside the dairy end of the building. Who knows what secrets were concealed in a chamber 10 feet square and 7 feet high found in a field where the plough had passed for many years?

The church in the centre of the village is dedicated to Saint Dubricius, a Celtic missionary and Bishop of Llandaff. It dates from the 13th century and has a peculiar truncated spire about which legends abound.

The ancient and well-known Ship Inn, like many of the cottages in the village, has a thatched roof and an unusual round chimney on the outside of the building. These cottages give Porlock its unique appearance and are much photographed by the present day visitors. The oldest building in Porlock – the 15th century Doverhay Manor – now houses a Museum and Information Centre. The village hall, with neither thatched roof nor picturesque chimneys, is nevertheless the centre of village life.

No description of Porlock, however brief, can fail to mention the red deer of Exmoor who run wild in the surrounding countryside and steal down at night to ravage gardens and flowers on graves in the cemetery. These noble creatures with handsome antlers and gentle faces can be met when out walking in the woods and are as much a part of the village scene as are the people.

Puriton ✤

It is difficult to visualise how parts of Puriton and Downend looked before the M5 cut through the land, remembering with a hint of nostalgia the lane where the first early violets were found, the hedgerows which yielded the biggest blackberries and Quarry Cottages.

Puriton's name was first believed to be Peritone, mentioned in the Domesday book 1086. For a small village it has a unique past. Its natural deposits provided work until the early 1960s. Tiles and the famous Bath Bricks were made. Stone was quarried, even salt was mined. When new roads and the M5 were built fascinating archaeological finds came to light.

Today new housing developments on old sites have taken place. Many trees have been planted on the old cement works, making this an attractive feature which can be seen when travelling either by train or road northbound.

The tower of Puriton church can be seen by travellers going west. The church is small but beautiful. The tower, chancel and chancel arch are early English. The nave was rebuilt at the beginning of the 15th century and the east wall was rebuilt about 1840. The lovely screen is late 15th century.

1987 saw a new school built in a lovely setting at the top of Rowlands Rise (The Rev Rowlands was once a vicar of Puriton). The old school which is probably over a hundred years old is being converted to private houses.

Just over the motorway bridge through Downend is Puriton's tiny hamlet of Dunball. This tiny wharf on the river Parrett was built in 1841, later another wharf was built now known as Bibbys. Dunball has been kept busy throughout its life with cargoes of coal from South Wales. Today huge cargoes of timber are brought from Russia. Tons of sand and gravel are also brought in from the Bristol Channel.

Pylle

The name Pylle means creek or haven. Poole in Dorset and Pill near Bristol are other spellings of the same word. This seems odd now that the village is thirty miles inland, but centuries ago when central Somerset was under water, with Glastonbury an island, the first settlement here was on the shoreline.

The original village has disappeared, probably wiped out by the Black Death plague. Only a few houses and the church stand round the village pond. In early spring the earth here is covered with snowdrops and is a beautiful sight. Later on wild daffodils and apple blossom provide a lovely setting for the little church. It was restored to its present state in Victorian days but the font and base of the tower are thought to be Saxon, and the tower itself is 14th century. It has five bells and some interesting carvings and iron work.

The other half of Pylle stands half a mile east on the A37. The old name for it was Street on the Fosse, being on the Fosse Way.

A school was built here and in the records of 1875 the schoolmaster complained that his 58 pupils were distracted from their lessons by passing traffic except when the windows frosted over. Numbers dropped so much that in 1958, with only 14 pupils, it closed. The building now provides an excellent village hall.

The village was part of the vast Portman estate, which owned land in several areas of Somerset and Dorset. Members of the family lived in Pylle Manor House and are buried in the churchyard. One was rector here, and restored the church.

Another link remaining with the Portman times is the way in which the older cottages are numbered. Each village on the estate started its house numbers from a different hundred. Pylle must have been eighth on the list, for they are 831, 853 and so on. If you know of other villages with impossibly large house numbers, it means that they were once on the Portman estate. There are several in Somerset and Dorset.

Pylle remains a small village as it is very difficult to get planning permission for new houses. So it is a quiet place except during June and July when thousands of people pass through on their way to the Royal Bath and West Show or the Glastonbury Pop Festival at Pilton.

Queen Camel ❦

The origin of the name Camel is not certain, but it may derive from the 'long narrow hill to the north of the church'. At the time of the Conquest, Queen Camel belonged to Countess Gytha, widow of Earl Godwin and mother of King Harold and the village remained Crown Property for nearly five centuries. The manor was often included in the Royal estates assigned to the Queens of England – hence the name. In 1558 Queen Mary gave the manor to Sir Walter Mildmay, in exchange for the manor of Little Weldon, Northants. His family retained the Lordship of Queen Camel until 1920–9 when the Mildmays sold the estate and thus ended nearly 400 years of ownership by the Mildmay family.

Queen Camel was always a place of note and by the mid 16th century was flourishing. There was a market twice a week and four fairs a year. Both linen and woollen cloth were made; several looms were situated in the main street, the cottagers doing the spinning in their own homes. At one time the cloth for the monks of Cleave was woven in Camel. The beautiful church is evidence of the prosperity of the parish and the village almost succeeded in achieving the status of a town.

However, on St Barnabas Eve, 1639, there was a disastrous fire from which Queen Camel never seemed to recover. The fire destroyed some 70 houses. Yet many of the cottages and houses in the main street today, are two to three hundred years old, some beautifully restored with stone from the local quarry and some with survivals of medieval origin. Hazelgrove House which became the manor house in the early 16th century, after an earlier manor was destroyed, is still in existence. In the past 15 years there has been considerable building with two new estates and conversion of the old tithe barn and the mill into dwellings; and the cobbled path leading to the church has been restored.

Now with the new developments and proximity of Yeovilton Royal Naval Air Station, there is a rapidly changing population. It was about 600 in 1670 and now tops 800. Local dialect has largely disappeared, the bus has replaced the taxi and traffic roars through the main street. Cricket and football are still played and bowls on the green given by Judge Armstrong. Happily there is still a commendable community spirit.

Rode

Rode is a pretty village of some 800 inhabitants, stretching down the gentle slope from St Lawrence's church to the river Frome and beyond to the old manor house, once occupied by the Batten-Poole family, but now the Tropical Bird Gardens. There are two theories about the name Rode; one is that it is derived from Rhyd, meaning ford; the other that it comes from Rood: a clearing in a forest, marked by a stake.

The village has been occupied for a long time. A pre-historic long barrow, called the Devil's Bed and Bolster lies not far from St Lawrence's church. The church was mentioned in the Domesday Book, although the present building is mainly 14th century. Rode is unusual because it has two parish churches in the village. The second, Christchurch, was built, along with a school, in Victorian times by Archdeacon Daubeney because the northern side of Rode was in Wiltshire and he did not want the families to worship in Somerset. Happily today all the village is in Somerset, but we are left with two churches.

There is also a strong non-conformist tradition in Rode (John Wesley preached here in 1746). Although in recent years the Methodists have decided to worship with the Baptists, the village school is still Methodist voluntary controlled.

At the time of the Napoleonic Wars at the beginning of the 19th century, 5000 people lived in Rode. The Frome valley was a busy, prosperous place with a cloth mill every half mile. There were two mills in Rode. Today there is little employment within the village. The mills have been silent for many years. The brewery no longer produces beer and is now a storage and distribution depot for Bass Charrington, employing less than 50 people. Agriculture provides work for a few, mainly in livestock farming including, a recent venture, snail farming. The number of shops has also declined dramatically from over twenty in the 1930s. With the closure of the general stores only the post office and a village shop are left.

Many people come to visit the Bird Gardens in Rode but others may recall the name because of a gruesome murder which took place at Langham House in 1860. It has been the subject of several books and a television programme. A young boy was murdered and his half-sister, Constance Kent, was convicted of the crime. Many people, however, believe her to have been innocent. Her father, an unpopular man, and his mistress, the children's nanny, are suspected.

Rodney Stoke ஜ௸

The small village of Rodney Stoke was once one of the homes of a very important English family who gave their name to it. Originally known as Stoke Giffard, it became Rodney Stoke when Richard de Rodney married Maud Giffard round about the year 1300. His son, Sir Walter, who succeeded him, owned many manors in Somerset, some of which are now in Avon and Bristol. He was a man of great importance, and held office as Sheriff of both Somerset and Dorset.

Unfortunately the manor no longer exists and there is only a small part of the porter's lodge still standing. It is used as a barn at Manor Farm (opposite the church) which was built on the site of the manor house.

Sir Edward Rodney loved his home at Rodney Stoke, as he gave the beautiful carved screen, dated 1625, the pulpit and font cover still to be seen in St Leonard's church. He was buried there, and the memorial to him and his wife, Lady Frances, are with others in the Rodney Chapel, the earliest dating from 1478. In 1885 Baron Rodney spent a considerable sum in repairing the memorials to his forebears, which results in a beautiful church, well worth a visit.

All the old houses are built of local stone, a dolomitic conglomerate which was quarried at Draycott and known as Draycott stone. This stone is unique to Draycott and was used in very early times, as it has been found in excavations of Roman buildings locally. It was quarried until the middle of this century and was used for many purposes, such as gate-posts, bridges and pillars, as well as for buildings. The front of Temple Meads station in Bristol is built of this pinky-hued stone. Not only was it used rough-hewn, but also a method of polishing it was devised, which resulted in 'Draycott Marble'. The largest piece of this is a polished table-top in Longleat House, measuring approximately 9 feet by 4 feet, but it was also used for memorials and gravestones.

St Audries 🌿

The village appears on the map as West Quantoxhead, but is more widely known as St Audries, after its church. Together with Weacombe, Lower Weacombe, Pitt, Staple and Rydon, it constitutes an area about the size of an ordinary large village. But sitting in the Quantock Hills at their northernmost end where hill and sea meet, it is far from ordinary in the views it encompasses, stretching over the Brendon Hills to Exmoor and Dunkery Beacon, and over the sea to the coast of Wales and the mountains beyond.

The original name was Cantocheve and, together with Weacombe, it is mentioned in the Domesday Book. The two manors continued to exist here under various owners until now, when Weacombe is still a family house and farm, but St Audries has become a public school for girls.

In the 16th century the name was changed to St Audries, the name being a corruption of St Etheldreda, the patron saint of the church. The church was rebuilt in the 19th century on the site of the old one, the only remains being a stone tomb and the slab of another dated 1433 which are in the crypt, a Norman font in the church and the remains of a churchyard cross. Though the church is small, it is richly decorated and has beautiful marble pillars of Devonshire stone. There is a ring of six bells in the tower, two of which are medieval.

The village, which originally clustered around manor and church, was moved southwards around Staple and Pitt. None of the old buildings have survived except parts of the House itself, but the new estate cottages and other houses built around the mid 19th century form part of the village as it is now.

Staple Farm is thought to have been built in the 17th century. At that time it was the custom to place into the walls of the building the remains of any black cat which died on the site. In the wall of the dining room there is still an elm box containing the bones of a cat found when redecoration was carried out recently.

As well as wool, the area has produced cider from its own orchards, but they are sadly all gone. The blacksmith still plies his trade, but his home, once a cider house, then the smithy's house, is now in private ownership and the smith himself comes from over the hill to shoe horses here twice a week. Vineyards once flourished on the hillside at Weacombe but they have been replaced by other crops.

Sampford Arundel

The village of Sampford Arundel lies at the western end of the Blackdown Hills, close to the Devon border and three miles from Wellington. At its centre is the parish church of the Holy Cross and the County Primary School.

Although a parochial school had been established by the Rev Barter Sweet many years earlier in 1835, it was not until 1880 that the Board School, set up under the 1870 Education Act opened on its present site.

A child attending school in the 1880s would have had to pay 2d a week. Let us eavesdrop on little Sophie, from Briar Cottage, Sampford Moor, as she tells about a morning in school one February:

'I have our school money tied up in the corner of my apron. There is 2d. each week for Dora and me and when James starts school Mother will have to find 1d. for him. Miss Hine collects the money. There are several children away today – the road to Peacy is flooded and there are

The village school at Sampford Arundel

more cases of measles. Nellie, who sits next to me and is my best friend, is away.

Vicar gives us all a Scripture lesson on the Parable of the Sower. Next we had to recite our tables and we got as far as twelve sevens are eighty four. We copied a poem from the blackboard on our slates – my slate squeaked a lot this morning. The little ones had their sand trays out and were practising some letters. I had put the primroses on Miss Hine's desk and last thing in the morning she gave us a Nature lesson on what we could find in the hedgerows in February.'

Sampford Arundel Primary School is today a happy, thriving village school with 78 children – their ages range from 4–11 years. The original building of 1880 still stands and is now the junior classroom. Various additions have been made over the years with the two caravan class-rooms being added recently.

Shapwick ✿

Shapwick is a small community with about 330 on the electoral roll, situated on the northern slopes of the Polden Hills. In former times it was a place of greater importance, being the senior parish of Shapwick with Ashcott and has always been the home of the vicar. It was mentioned in the Domesday Book.

The first church was out of the village in a field now called Old Church near Beerway Farm but the present church was built in its central position and consecrated in 1331. It is well maintained today with much love and care with a wonderful collection of modern hassocks made by the ladies of the village. There is a peal of 6 bells which are rung regularly.

The village has the unusual distinction of having two manor houses, two dovecotes and two ice-houses. In the 19th century it was the most popular of the Polden Hill spas with an elaborate pump room near Northbrook Farm, of which sadly no trace survives today. There is also a heronry in one of the woods.

The village was the site of the murder of St Indractus and his companions who were on a pilgrimage to Glastonbury. A legend exists that a light shines over the place where the bodies were buried and three haloes have been seen shining in the annexe to Shapwick House within living memory.

Today there is no industry in the village, the last of which, Barnett's Joinery, closed in 1982 and the factory site was demolished in 1987 for housing development. There is still an old watermill converted into a dwelling and there are records of a windmill on the hill to the south of the village. There was also a malthouse and two quarries for blue lias stone of which most of the village is built. Although many of the farms had their own cider presses, the cider house (now the vicar's room) was a communal press for the village.

Lord Vesty bought the Warry's estate but not their home, Shapwick House, in 1943 and that of the Strangways of the manor in 1944 and thus all the farms and most of the land and houses within the parish boundary. Some of the land and houses have since been sold off but it still remains largely an estate village. The present Lord Vesty is absentee landlord and patron of the church.

Shepton Beauchamp ❧

Shepton Beauchamp lies two miles west of South Petherton, an attractive, mainly agricultural village. It is almost unique in that it has an old fives court wall, only seven of which are left in the County of Somerset. The original game was said to have been first played against church walls but, to protect them, individual fives walls were built. Today it is not played at any of the venues but the walls themselves are a monument to bygone days. The ball finials which top the wall are a significant reminder that the game could not be played without a leather ball and it is thought that it needed five members in a team to play. Who knows, maybe the game will return in the years ahead.

The fives wall in Shepton Beauchamp belongs to the village and was repaired a few years ago by Somerset County Council.

Egg shackling is a very old custom shrouded in mystery and very little is known as to why it is carried out or for how long it has been done. On Shrove Tuesday the children of Barrington and Shepton Beauchamp take eggs to school. These are then placed in a container (in Shepton it is a garden sieve) which is gently shaken and the eggs removed as they crack, the winner being the last uncracked egg left in the sieve. Prizes are awarded and in Shepton Beauchamp the money for the prizes was left to the village by a Mr F. Robins, who died in 1934.

Shipham 🐑

The name of a village often reveals its past. This is true of Shipham. In the Domesday Book entry, the village is called Sipeham, which is Saxon for sheep hamlet. Nine hundred years later, there are still sheep on the hills.

Bordering the green is the Miners' Arms, which recalls another part of Shipham's history. From the mid-16th century until the 1830s, mining of calamine (zinc ore) was an important source of income in Shipham, Rowberrow and Star. Miners, from near and far, came to teach the craft and work in the industry. They worked in grooves, so the area was described as groovy ground. Hence the name 'gruffy ground' as the old mining fields are now called. The miners were said to be an unruly lot. As they earned more than the shepherds, there were frequent disagreements and fighting between the two groups. Their extra money was often spent on heavy drinking which increased the disorderliness.

Hannah More, a Bristol philanthropist, disturbed by reports of the sad state of the women and children, came, with her sisters, to Shipham and was greatly shocked. As a result, they opened a Sunday and day school in 1790. There are families in the village now, who own a handed-down Hannah More Bible. When she died in 1833, a National School replaced hers and in 1855 one was built in Rowberrow. A new school was built in 1973.

During the mining years, the population rose to over a thousand, later dwindling – mostly in Rowberrow – to half this. As the result of building on the outskirts of the village in the 1960s, the inhabitants again number over a thousand. This is not likely to increase, as the district has been declared an area of outstanding natural beauty, and further building is discouraged. The West Mendip Way from Wells to Uphill, goes through Shipham and this and the country lanes and forest paths bring ramblers and riders to the area.

Being a compact village, our social life has been less affected by change than some straggling communities, although the closely-knit relationship of earlier days is absent. However, there is plenty of social life for those who want it, and services of a post office, shops and garages. Three inns and two hotels cater for some of the villagers and the tourists who visit.

Mining history came dramatically to the fore again in 1979, when there was concern about the level of cadmium in the soil, brought to the surface by mining, and the possible health hazard involved. After checking health, food, air and gardens, the authorities gave the village a clean bill of health, and the 'Cadmium Scare' faded into the background.

144

Somerton 🌿

Somerton made its major impact on the map of England in the 7th century when it was the administrative centre for this part of the Saxon kingdom of Wessex. Its name was extended to the people in the area it controlled and this area became known as Somerset, although Somerton soon ceased to be the most important settlement and never grew into a large town. It is a lovely place with a wide market square surrounded by old stone houses and an octagonal, roofed Market Cross as a focal point at the centre.

The church is quite plain on the outside but inside is one of the finest wooden carved roofs in the county. It is shallow pitched with massive, richly decorated tie beams and short king posts. The whole area of the roof is divided into square carved panels set in the framework of the structural timbers which are decorated with carved bosses where they intersect. There are 640 panels each carved with the same quatrefoil design but the bosses have many patterns and even include a cider barrel. In the triangular spaces above each beam are the chief glory of the roof, 22 fantastic and monstrous dragons facing each other in pairs, superbly designed and executed.

Before the days of National Insurance and the Health Service, Provident Societies were important in most rural communities. Somerton Men's Club, one of these, flourished for over a century. Every summer there was a Club Day which was a local holiday with a church service, processions and a fair in the market square.

Somerton has almost doubled in size during the last 25 years but it has not lost its community spirit and still retains a village atmosphere.

South Cadbury 🌿

Cadbury Castle is one of the finest Iron Age Camps in Somerset, extending over some 18 acres. In a field to the west many bones of men and boys have been found – probably Britons killed by the Saxons. A hoard of Roman coins was found in 1922.

Cadbury is so impressive that it is no wonder that it is identified in folklore with Camelot and King Arthur and his Knights. At the foot of the hill, making its way towards Glastonbury is a track marked 'King Arthur's Hunting Causeway'.

South Cheriton & Horsington 🎨

Travelling south from Wincanton along the A357, one comes to the pretty conservation village of South Cheriton, its most notable feature being the old Toll House – a delightful, bow-fronted building on the main road, dating from 1824. It is unusual in that the original tariff board, which makes interesting reading is still in place.

Passing through the meandering street of the village, past houses and cottages of all ages, some as old as 400 years, one reaches the farmland mostly used for dairy cattle. One of the fields is known as Butts Field (many of the fields have names) and this is because it was once used for archery practise, as evidenced by the finding of many an ancient arrow head. The field is long and very narrow, and bordered by thick hedges.

One is now in the flat land known as the Horsington Marsh, and Horsington village nestles at the foot of a gentle slope. The Marsh seems to have a being of its own. Sometimes it is dark, brooding, sometimes bright and stark as on those crisp winter days when you stand bathed in deceptive sunlight. Then there are those warm summer days when the Marsh looks half asleep, but hiding beneath that sleepy look are millions of flying, running, creeping, scurrying creatures that have to make hay while the sun shines. The snow when it comes lies deep on the Marsh for days, blanketing the field and hiding the hedges, so all look like a crumpled white counterpane. When the snow melts, or the rain has slanted across the Marsh for days, it changes again to what looks like large sheets of glass, mirroring the sky. The most fascinating of all, are the days when the Marsh has disappeared beneath the autumn mists, with here and there tree-tops dotted like islands on the surface.

South Petherton 🎨

South Petherton is a large village, by-passed by the main road. Its name is derived from the 'tun' by the river Parrett. It is traditionally an agricultural community, with some flax-growing and glove-making in the last century.

The oldest and perhaps one of the most beautiful buildings in South Petherton is the manor house (King Ina's Palace) constructed of honey-coloured local Hamstone and so-called because it was reputedly built on the site of one of the hunting lodges of King Ina of Wessex. He was the

South Petherton Manor House, known as King Ina's Palace

Saxon king who had his capital at Somerton and who founded the present County Town of Taunton in AD 718.

An effigy was found nearby, believed to be of Sir Philip D'Albini who died in about 1292. This effigy is of Hamstone and represents a very beautiful young man in chain mail and it now rests in the parish church of St Peter and St Paul in South Petherton.

The house has now been divided into three separate dwellings and various cottages, lodges and parcels of land sold off. The present dwellings are the right wing, the west wing and a small cottage formed from what was formerly the chapel and part of what used to be the servants' quarters.

Two colourful village characters, probably born just before the First World War, were Gwen and Sis, the result of the seduction of a respectable village maiden by a farmer's son from a neighbouring village who repudiated his paternity! Now gone, they were two truly compassionate women, who are greatly missed.

They were well-known characters on the roads between South Petherton, Shepton Beauchamp and Crewkerne where they would go to get animal feed. They despised modern ways and traffic and would drive in the middle of the road, hitching their equipage to 'No Waiting' signs in Crewkerne, and when Petherton Square was made a one-way system would drive down the wrong side as a matter of principle; their invariable answers were 'Osses were 'ere afore cars' or 'Oss can't read'. The traffic tailed back for miles, and strong men would pale at their choice of expletives if challenged to moved over!

Spaxton ❧

Spaxton is spread out over a network of country lanes, partly on the main street, partly on side lanes. Four Forks is the lower part of Spaxton. The buildings, which were once the Agapemone – The Abode of Love – are on the left near the Lamb Inn. The Agapemonite religious sect formed by Rev Prince, the curate of the hamlet of Charlynch in the 1840s, continued for some decades. Victorian society was scandalised by what they imagined was 'going on' behind the high stone walls and the speculation did not cease until the sale of the property in the late 1950s.

In Spaxton main street the post office juts into the roadway. Beyond, the garage is sited where the 18th century wheelwright, carpenter, millwright, undertaker and blacksmith plied their trades. Only the blacksmith remains nearby, but the 20th century car has replaced the 19th century farm-cart and carriage.

The lower part of Spaxton peters out and fields line the road until we reach the village hall (1940) and playing fields (1957), much valued by village organisations. The main hall has a fine dance floor made of narrow oak strips which were the only wood available at the start of the war. A new village hall would have to pay dear for such a floor in these days! A few yards on is Spaxton school, built in 1860 by Henry Labouchere.

Lanes lead off the main road. Splatt Lane leads past the almshouses (endowed 1668–1708 by Rev Cook) to the parish church of St Margaret whose later English architecture is crowned by a peal of six bells. Court Farm a step further on is a lovely cluster of farmhouse and outbuildings. Alongside this old mill, mill-pond and race are part of a delightful garden. Nearby is a genuine 'cottage industry', internationally known for its preserves.

Most of the land and property in the area was held from 1100–1681 by the Malet family, being mentioned in the Domesday Book (1086).

From 1100 until 1919 the estate was in the hands of only three families. The whole estate was then sold and for the first time in over 800 years many local farmers and cottagers took the opportunity to buy their farms and houses.

Staple Fitzpaine, Bickenhall & Curland

Staple Fitzpaine, Bickenhall and Curland are three small villages, grouped together under the shadow of Castle Neroche. They are well wooded areas of mixed, mainly dairy farming. Staple and Bickenhall (Bichehalle) were mentioned in the Domesday Book. Staple means pillar or marking post, in this case the very large stone near Staple church, which the Devil is supposed to have thrown at the church from Castle Beacon. Curland means Curry Land – the church there having been a chapel of ease attached to Curry Mallet.

All three villages had stone churches built in the 12th century, but sadly, only the beautiful church of St Peter's, Staple Fitzpaine, now remains in use. The tower is considered to be the most beautiful small tower in a county of beautiful towers. It has a rich battlemented crown and an exuberance of pinnacles and gargoyles. There is a Norman archway at the south door.

The Portman family were associated with Staple for over 400 years. In 1643 Sir William Portman built an almshouse or hospital for 6 poor people, who were expected to attend church in a green wool cloth gown and cap and if they did not attend they were fined 4 pennies. This building still stands in the centre of the village, but has been up-dated to make 4 very pleasant, self-contained units for elderly people – not now forced to attend the church!

Between 1830 and 1861 there were three schools in the vicinity, with a total of almost 100 pupils, because the cottages were filled with farm workers and their children. Now the village school is closed and the few remaining children travel, by bus, to Thurlbear, Hatch Beauchamp or Monckton Heathfield.

There used to be an inn, called The Ragged Cat, at Brandy Bridge, on the river Rag at Bickenhall. The next bridge down the river is called Bottle Bridge. Rab Channing used to bring smuggled spirits here, from

Lyme Regis and he had a terrific fight with the Excise men. The Excise men also looked for butter and a pig at Verrier's cottage (now called Orchard House), in Curland. They were treated to a drink of cider from a cask with a false bottom – the pig being hidden in the other end; and the old woman pleading rheumatism, sat on the vat of butter, covering it with her voluminous skirts!

Staplegrove ༄

Staplegrove lies 1½ miles north-west of the county town of Taunton. The earliest documentary evidence goes back 500 years.

Although mainly a residential area today, it was in the 18th century a typical hamlet, having a blacksmith, a butcher, a storekeeper and a Dame School. Later more commerce was introduced and by 1861 a silk mill, powered by water rising at Crowcombe in the Quantock hills, was thriving together with another mill powered by a rivulet rising at Hestercombe. Large quantities of flax were grown in the area. The local doctor was very enterprising, he owned a large property Fairwater House (now part of Taunton School) which he ran as a lunatic asylum for gentlewomen.

Nowadays the post office still stands in what the local residents call the 'village', which differentiates between the new developments in the Bindon Road area, where light industrial units and stores combine with a mixture of council and privately owned properties.

The parish had a school attached to the church until recent times. Now the old school is a house and a new school has been built in the more densely populated area of Bindon Road.

There are still some farms surviving whose names have not changed since the 15th century ie Yallands, Pomeroys and Burlands (which has now diversified into a thriving vineyard).

The church dates back to 1308 when it was a mere chapelry, part of the huge priory of St James. There are squint windows in the main tower where lepers were allowed to peer in during the service. The tower has 5 bells, side aisles and vestry being added in the 19th century.

The Grove from which the village takes its name consists of oak, ash elm and lime trees. During the mid 1970s many of the elm trees had to be cut down because of Dutch Elm disease, but these have been replaced.

Staplehay ❧

Probably the most striking difference between Staplehay now and in the early part of the century is that instead of being a village in its own right, it has become part of the larger village of Trull, which in turn has become a suburb of Taunton two miles away. Eighty years ago Staplehay had its own bakery, where villagers could roast their Sunday joints, a slaughter-house and butchery, two cobblers, a dressmaker, a carpenter and under-taker, a public house and a school. The public house, the Crown Inn, still flourishes, and the butcher's premises still exist, though converted into an attractive house. The schoolroom is now the garage of the large house known as Staplehay Cross, which years ago was the manse for the chapel in Fulwood about two miles away towards the next village of Blagdon Hill. But there are no longer any shops left, and the nearest cobblers, dressmakers and undertakers are in Taunton 2½ miles away.

Driving into Taunton along the busy Honiton Road it is hard to imagine that years ago the only way to get there was on foot or horseback, or in the carrier's cart which drove in once a week from Blagdon Hill.

The road itself was made of flint stones quarried at Blagdon Hill. These were offloaded at various points, and two stone-crackers, Mr Shepherd and Mr Hayes, sat on sacking at the roadside wearing goggles, leather aprons and protective mittens, breaking the stones into small pieces. Sacking stretched between poles kept flying splinters of flint from hurting passers-by. The stones were put into orderly heaps which were measured to gauge payment for the work.

Little is left of the old Staplehay, except a group of cottages known as Wayside which must have been the heart of the village, occupied by farmworkers, the stone-crackers and other artisans. The cottages have been updated inside, but have retained their outward appearance. Other old houses are still to be found, though they are mostly surrounded by more modern dwellings and large housing developments.

Stawell ❧

Stawell is recorded in the Domesday Book. The name probably comes from the Saxon words for 'Stoney stream' or 'Well', and may allude to the pond at Ford Farm. Objects which lie in this pond become encrusted with lime.

A feature of the village is the little church perched high above its stone boundary walls. It is believed that the churchyard was built up with soil from neighbouring woodland to avoid flooding. This may well be true, as the capitals of the pillars facing you on entering the church are certainly low in height.

According to local legend, a peal of bells was promised by a benefactor to either Moorlynch or Stawell, whichever had the most births and deaths in a year. Stawell villagers became so confident that they began building the tower, but were beaten at the last minute. They were so despondent that the tower was abandoned and just roofed over.

There is an unusual stone pavement running around the perimeter of the south and west boundary walls along Ford Lane, joining with the old coffin path through the grounds of the Grange and on to Chilton Polden.

The Grange in Ford Lane, Stawell

152

Stawell is one of the seven churches that came under the jurisdiction of the abbot of Glastonbury. The Grange, a beautiful old house in Ford Lane is where the abbot resided on his visits to these churches.

Stawell has still managed to retain its rural character, and is now known for picking your own apples in tranquil orchards.

Stogursey ✍️

If you wish to visit a failed medieval town – come to Stogursey. There is a Norman castle and Priory church, a stone butter cross stands near the old market square and 'The Angelus Bell' still tolls 'Ding Dong Darling Mary Sparking' from the almshouse's bell tower.

Stogursey is the Anglicised name from the Norman, Stoke Courcy, the manor being held by William de Courcy.

The Priory church was built in 1100 by the Benedictine monks from Lonlay L'Abbaye in Normandy and the link was re-forged in 1986 by the Twinning Association.

This rural area lies between the Quantock Hills and the Bristol Channel. The dairy farms have changed to corn production and the cider apple orchards are dwindling.

Piercing the skyline is the stately Victorian Gothic School built as 'A Thank Offering by Sir P. P. F. P. Acland Bart., AD 1860' for the recovery of his daughter Isobel. The school and playgroup have over 100 pupils from within a five mile radius.

The sound of the horn, the cry of the hounds and the clatter of hoofs – the West Somerset Vale Hounds are in full cry along the lanes and across the fields! The kennels are on Farringdon Hill Top.

Bridgwater Bay is a National Nature Reserve of 6,500 acres of mud flats and salt marshes. Many ducks and waders winter here. The sight of 10,000 dunlin in dipping ribbon flight flashing over the shore is a 'shining glory'. As many as 5,000 widgeon graze on the saltings and shellduck moult there in summer. Yellow horned poppies grow along the shingle ridge.

Hinkley Point Power Station (Nuclear) stands four square on the Severn Shore. This great industry has revitalised the district and 'C' Station is planned to supply the national electricity needs of the 1990s.

At Stolford there has been 'slid' fishing since the 15th century. The last two fishermen, Tony Brewer and Brendan Sellick, traverse the mud shore for 1½ miles aided by the Stolford Mud Horse, a slid, a unique wooden sledge, which they push out strongly to slide it over the mud to collect their catch. Cone-shaped nets attached to tall poles catch shrimps, prawns, skate and eels.

Stoke St Gregory ✒

Just off the A361 lies the village of Stoke St Gregory – once described as being a pleasant place on the way to nowhere.

The village, one of the largest in Somerset, covers an area of around 3,967 acres and took its name from the church dedicated to Gregory the Great.

It is situated on the Somerset Levels, which for centuries has been the centre of withy growing and basket making. The willow tree flourishes naturally on the wetlands of Somerset and it was discovered that the young straight shoots could be twisted, plaited and woven into many useful articles. The village is now part of the Withy Trail and welcomes holiday makers each year who flock to see the displays provided by the local growers and to buy the withy products.

Present day Stoke St Gregory is a study in contrasts – the quiet beauty of the leafy lanes – the rattle of the tractors – the rumble of the occasional bus and also the piercing shriek of a jet plane passing overhead. The village has flourished over the years. It has a thriving school, which celebrates Egg Shackling each Pancake Day. It is also still lucky enough to have two shops and a post office, as well as three pubs, a guest house and numerous bed and breakfast residences. The church, Baptist chapel and village hall provide facilities and activities that may be enjoyed by all.

Stoke St Michael ✒

Stoke St Michael, situated on the Mendip Hills, is within walking distance of the Beacon Hill, one of the highest points.

In very early documents the village was called Stockland or Stoke Lane, but it is within the last two or three decades that Stoke St Michael has become used more than the less attractive Stoke Lane. The St Michael is taken from the parish church.

In AD 926 the monks of Glastonbury built a chapel and dedicated it to 'The Glory of God and St Michael and all Angels'. A Norman church was later built on the same site and in 1438 was replaced by an early English style church. In 1901 much interior alteration was done.

There is a large farming community around the village and farmers made their own cheese until about 1912 when a small milk factory was established here. This was later enlarged and cheese made until it closed in 1926.

In the past there have been sawyards, tanyards and mills for making edge tools and paper. A corn mill at the bottom of Mill Lane was operated by the stream which runs through the centre of the village.

Stoke St Michael has always been surrounded by quarries. The nearest one is Moonshill Quarry, John Wainwright & Co. It extends over a large area and from it is extracted basalt which is turned into chippings and tarmacadam on the site.

At one time there were three bakers in the village, baking bread in old fashioned faggot ovens and delivering it by horse and trap. There were four shops and three public houses. There is now only one pub, a grocery store, butcher's shop, post office and general store with petrol station.

The only public house is the Knatchbull Arms, built in the finest example of 17th century architecture. Stoke's claim to fame is, that in 1942 at the Knatchbull Arms there was the largest secret assembly of high ranking Officers and Generals in the history of the country, including Lord Montgomery and Lord Wavell.

The old school, built in 1837, was maintained by voluntary subscription and school pence before being taken over by the County Council. It is now closed. The large new school built on the outside of the village is fully equipped with the latest facilities for school use.

In 1977 The Unicorn Glass Workshop was established in part of 15th century Tooses Farm by Fran Johnston. Beautiful stained glass windows are designed and made there, also lovely birds, animals and flowers for window decoration. Visitors are always welcome by appointment.

Stoke-sub-Hamdon 🌿

Stoke-sub-Hamdon actually consists of two manors in one civil parish – West Stoke (Stoca or Stocke) and East Stoke (Stocket). West Stoke is the main village nestling under Hamdon Hill which accounts for part of the name, of course, but Stoke is more difficult to pin down. It is of Viking origin and has many meanings – 'Holy Place' is one of them and may account for the parish church being aloof from the village, perhaps on a

Celtic site. It dates from about 1100 and contains all architectural styles from Norman to late perpendicular with some Jacobean furnishings. It is a delightful small church and has a stained glass window depicting the main industries of farming, quarrying and gloving.

Ham Hill was made a Country Park by 1970; much to its detriment in the opinion of many villagers. The quarrying was, of course, carried out on the Hill and the lovely Hamstone was used to build large houses, the Chapels, cottages and, in fact, council estates. An interesting custom was that in the 17th century the Ham Hill quarrymen and masons kept their own court to look after the working rights of the men. The industry recorded John Dore and Partners in the early 15th century and stonework still continues today.

Apart from this source of employment, the farms played a great part in the prosperity of the village, and great flocks of sheep could be seen grazing on the hill. Now, alas, only four farms remain, mostly arable, and only one has a herd of cows. However, the industry which perhaps has influenced the welfare of the inhabitants to the greatest extent is the gloving industry. It was brought to Stoke in the 18th century and at one time there were as many as seven factories. The remaining largest manufacturer of this number became a private family company in 1847.

At the present time, Stoke has both a cricket and football team and, between the two World Wars, was famous for organising comic football matches which are remembered as hilarious events. Stoke is also proud of its village band, which started as a military band in 1891 and is the only village band in Somerset to have competed at the Royal Albert Hall.

Ston Easton

Ston Easton is a rather scattered village on the main Bristol to Shepton Mallet road. The residence of Ston Easton Park was purchased from the Crown in the reign of Henry VIII for £500 by one John Hippisley. The last owner of that family was Commander R. J. B. Hippisley.

The Commander gave a field to the village which is used as a general playing field by the Cricket Club, Tennis Club and any organisation that may want to hold an outdoor function. This field is adjacent to the former Red Room (village hall) with its skittle alley and Working Men's Club.

In the High Street was the village general stores and sub-post office kept by the Elford family, and then Gaits the builders and undertakers and lastly the Speed's off-licence. A little further along is the lovely church which dates back to Norman times.

The other important residence was Clare Hall, originally owned by Mrs Ivan Hippisley. About 60 years ago, it was reputed that it was haunted by a ghost called 'The Grey Lady' because she wore a grey cloak with a hood.

Ston Easton estate together with the farms provided the main source of employment for the villagers.

What about the village now? Despite the fact that the shop, sub-post office, builder's yard, off-licence and regular bus service no longer exist, it is very much alive.

Ston Easton Park was bought by William Rees-Mogg after the death of Commander Hippisley and is now owned by Peter Smedley, grandson of the originator of Smedley's tinned vegetables. It is reputed to be the best hotel of its kind in the country. It is a quiet retreat for the famous and wealthy. Clare Hall is now a first-class nursing home and the company Penny's Plant Hire now exists on the site of Mr Penny's late grandfather's smallholding.

So there are three good sources of employment, not forgetting several farms, in the village.

Stratton on the Fosse &

It is likely that Stratton began as an outpost in Roman times on the Fosse Way, which ran from Lincoln to Exeter. Stratton, spelt 'Strattone' was the name given then to the flat stones used for paving, and 'fosse' meant ditch.

The manor of Strattone was part of the Abbey of Glastonbury until, according to the Domesday Book it was given by William the Conqueror to his chaplain, the Bishop of Constances in Normandy. The Bishop is reputed to have rebuilt the parish church, and dedicated it to St Vigor, a 6th century saint much revered by the Normans, and who was Bishop of Bayeux from AD 513–537. There is only one other church in England at Fulborne, near Cambridge, dedicated to this Saint.

Following harassment during the French Revolution the Community of St Gregory at Douai in Flanders moved to England and settled here at the beginning of the 19th century. Today Downside Monastery has developed into a leading Catholic school for boys, with 500 pupils, nearly all boarders, and with Downside Abbey at its centre standing out on the skyline.

The coal pits are now all closed, but a few elderly men can still tell of a lifetime of work in them. It was a hard life for these men of Mendip – the coal seams are shaped like the sides of a saucer, too steep and shallow for modern equipment and therefore uneconomical to mine by present standards.

As well as coal mining, villagers in the past were involved in farming, quarrying, building and small business. One school, in the 1890s was run by a husband and wife. He was also the village baker. His wife taught needlework, but often had to look after the whole school while he saw to his baking. Sometimes when the older boys appeared to be getting out of hand, she would send for him, and he would arrive in haste, his hands covered in flour, to deal with the situation! The children were keen to take messages to him just when the bread was leaving the oven, in the hope of a tasty sample.

The present school, the only one remaining, is soon to close, and there are plans to build a new one near the boundary to serve both Stratton and Chilcompton.

The Manor of Stratton had passed to the Gurney family in 1297, but was confiscated from them following their involvement in the murder of Edward II in 1327, and it became part of the property of the Duchy of Cornwall. Today this consists of 700 acres in four holdings. As part of the scheme encouraged by Prince Charles, the old stone barn at Fosse Farm has been converted into 2 workshops producing toys and leather accessories.

Tatworth ✖

On the borders of Somerset, Dorset and Devon is the village of Tatworth. Tatworth had no parish church until the last century, has no village green, duck pond or centre and although it is made up of a number of very ancient settlements and hamlets, it appears as unremarkable as any village could be. It claims neither to be the birthplace of national heroes nor eminent scholars and has no castle, great house or natural wonder.

Tatworth does have just one claim to fame, an event unique in Great Britain, the yearly meeting of Stowell Court. Legend and local gossip have it that some thirty villagers who have a 'right' in Stowell meadow meet yearly on the first Tuesday after the first Saturday after the 6th of

April in a secret room at Ye Olde Poppe Inne on the outskirts of Tatworth to bid for the use of Stowell meadow for the coming year.

Regulars at the Poppe Inn who have no access to the court will tell visitors that in the secret room behind locked doors members of the court make their bids for the meadow while a lighted candle burns and that they accept the last bid before the candle flickers out. The custom is, they say, that a supper of bread, Dorset Blue cheese, watercress and beer is laid out while the candle burns and that while the flame still glows no member there can rise from his seat.

Much of the local lore surrounding Stowell Court will not, of course, bear too close a scrutiny, but the real history of the ceremony goes back to the feudal use of land in the 11th century. Then most estates or villages were farmed on an open field system with land set aside for common grazing, watermeadows and woodlands.

By 1819 all land in Tatworth had been enclosed but Stowell meadow of six acres, well watered and sheltered, was still 'common', where several farmers in Tatworth were entitled to pasture their cattle. The farmers concerned met together and decided to let the meadow yearly to the highest bidder, dividing the rent received among those with ancient rights.

The meadow, about a half mile to the north of the inn, is one of the last of the ancient water meadows, and having never been ploughed or treated with pesticides or chemical fertilisers, is the home of many wild plants found but rarely today. Such an interesting meadow has attracted the interest of the Nature Conservancy and it is hoped that soon the meadow will be designated a Site of Special Scientific Importance.

Templecombe

In 1987 Templecombe won first prize in British Rail's Small Station Category (keeping company with Waterloo who won in the Biggest). It functions with only two signalmen (besides reliefs) who work the signals, issue the tickets, tend the flowers, and sweep the platforms. They are based in the old signal box housing 64 levers, now reduced to 16, but accommodating also ticket office and waiting room, all upstairs!

Templecombe Station Working Committee, chaired by Ian Matthews, whose boyhood ambition had been to work on the railway, slaved for its reopening. A trial stop on Sunday, 5th September 1982, picked up 270 passengers, and crowds of us watched them set off for a trip to Paignton.

St Mary's Church, Templecombe

Then on 3rd October 1983 the station was officially opened. As a special tribute to untiring efforts the nameplate 'Templecombe' was unveiled on diesel locomotive 33122 on Saturday 31st October 1987 – in pouring rain!

In St Mary's church, although the Norman tower and font, the waggon roof of the nave, and the seats by the west door 'the narrowest seats in Christendom' have for long been of interest, it is the painting on the south wall that has been attracting attention.

In 1945, outside one of Mrs Topp's cottages beside the Blue Boar, one of her tenants, Mrs Drew, noticed a face painted on wood in the rafters of a lean-to shed. The then Rector took possession, though it was not until 1956 that the panel was hung in the church. It seems that this is a medieval painting which may be a copy of the figure on the Turin Holy Shroud.

There is speculation regarding its possible connection with the Knights Templar, who, from 1186 until the Order was suppressed in 1312, had their preceptory on the site of the present manor house, one of the oldest buildings in the village.

Twentieth century changes are many. The farming industry has been revolutionised. Out of nearly twenty farms milking cows, today there are only three. The Empire Game Farm produces pheasants and partridges for shooting and conservation. The old Rectory Farm is now enlarged as Knights Templar Court, a residential home for 24 elderly men and women, yet preserving a little of its former site in keeping milking goats, poultry and donkeys.

The Royal Hotel is our only public house now, though the new Recreation and Sports Club runs a bar with skittles and social events, and outside there are two hard tennis courts, and, at last, a *level* soccer pitch!

Thornfalcon ✍

This is a small rural village situated about 4 miles east of Taunton. The village is somewhat scattered as there is no main street and the farmhouses and other dwellings are spread throughout the area. Other major lines of communication at one time ran through the parish, a canal from Taunton to Chard and also a branch railway line serving the same two towns but these have now been closed. The population in 1911 was recorded as being 161, but has declined since then.

There has been a church on the present site since the second half of the 13th century and the first known rector was Simon de Insula appointed during November 1265. Most of the datable part of the present building are the result of extensive alterations from the late 14th century onwards.

There is a stone memorial cross at the junction of Church Lane and this was a temporary resting place for coffins of members of the Chisholm Batten family en route from their family home Court House to the church. The dates of the funerals are inscribed on the sides of the base of the cross which is situated approximately halfway between the residence and church.

To the east of the parish the ground rises to a broken ridge, the predominant feature being a hill with a clump of trees on top known as 'Thorn Hill'. At times of national celebrations this has for a number of years been the site for a bonfire. The last occasion was the marriage of the Prince of Wales and Lady Diana Spencer on 29th July 1981.

Tintinhull ✒

Steeped in history the village of Tintinhull lies close to the Fosse Way (A303), betwixt Ilchester and Ilminster. There are many derivations of its name but one is the Saxon 'to tan' which signifies to examine or speculate.

The Hundred of Tintinhull came about when King Alfred divided the counties into hundreds. The whole hundred including the village of its name was given by William Earl of Morton to the monks of Montacute. The monks had a free warren here and a market and fair. In later years the tithes, manor and advowson united and in the 17th century were owned by the Napper family. The old Hundred green still exists with the whipping stone used as a punishment but the stocks have been moved to the entrance to St Margaret's church and the horse pool has been filled in and is now a car park.

Many of the beautiful houses are built of Hamstone once quarried from nearby Ham Hill. Fine examples of architecture include The Court, Tintinhull House and The Dower House which were once all owned by the Napper family. The Court was formerly The Parsonage but this did not mean that it was The Vicarage. When the Nappers became lay rectors they lived in the house. Once a mansion, Tintinhull House was given to the National Trust in 1954.

St Margaret's church dating back to the early 13th century has several interesting features. The Jacobean pulpit has a canopy and there are brasses of two 15th century rectors and the Nappers. Benches made in 1511–12 have hinged flaps upon which sat the servants. When repairs to the churchyard wall were made in 1518, stone was brought from the ruins of Montacute Castle.

When village schools were closing in Somerset we were fortunate in having a larger school built on glebe land, replacing the two-classroom building which still stands in Church Street but is now converted into a family house.

Primarily an agricultural community, gloving has been a dominant craft and there are records of deeds specifying a pair of gloves in lieu of rent as far back as Edward I. Much employment was provided in 1880 when Robert Southcombe founded a glove factory which still carries on in the family tradition.

An ancient Church Day of the village was the Tingel Feast. Extending over a week, each day had a different event. There was much sporting, eating and drinking and the Feast was fixed for centuries for the first Monday following Sunday after the 1st of May. From the Feast evolved 'Club Day' whose Friendly Society rules date from 1843. Sadly this event has lapsed but we often enjoy a Village Carnival Week.

Trull 🌿

From the early 16th century our village became known as Trull (hopefully no connection with the dictionary definition of the word) and was derived from the Old English 'trendle', meaning a ring or circle. Trull nestles in the lovely Vale of Taunton Deane sheltered by the Quantocks, the Blackdowns and Cotlake Hill.

The church, dedicated to All Saints, has been the centre of village life for at least 700 years. Beautiful is an inadequate word to describe the building which is famous for its carved woodwork. The rood screen has fan vaulting and the wooden pulpit is one of the most remarkable of the many ancient pulpits in the West of England, with its carved figures. Much of the seating is ancient and some uncomfortable but this is more than compensated by the exquisitely carved benchends, one of which is dated 1570.

Maybe Trull's most widely-known personality was Juliana Horatio Ewing, a prolific writer of stories and poems chiefly for children in the last century. She is buried in Trull churchyard close to the old stocks under the large yew tree. Her husband Colonel Alexander Ewing composed the well-known tune to the hymn 'Jerusalem the Golden'. Trull's reputed longest lived inhabitant was Mrs Elizabeth Broadmead who died in 1783 at the age of 115.

There is a record of a school in Trull as long ago as 1623. About 1755 John Wyatt's Charity School was established in a room by the church near where the war memorial now stands with accommodation above for the schoolmaster. This school must have continued until 1875 when land was conveyed to 'the Minister and Churchwardens for the building of a school' on the present site. In 1880 a Government Inspector recommended the appointment of an assistant as 'it was difficult for the master to cope with 132 children of all ages'! The school has been extensively improved over the years but still remains a Church of England Voluntary Aided school and pupils leaving the school are presented with bibles from the proceeds of the John Wyatt Charity to this day.

Until recent reorganisation of parish boundaries there was no pub in

Trull but traces remain of ale houses such as Fairlawn Cottage where residents brought their jugs to be filled through a hole in the wall and Lilac Cottage where there is still visible evidence of barrels being rolled in and out.

No great family has ever lived in Trull and there was never a resident lord of the manor. There are however some very picturesque old houses such as King's Gatchell and Trull Green Farm.

Some families have lived in the village for generations but generally Trull has a changing population. New houses stand cheek by jowl with old, renovations go apace and a warm welcome awaits the new arrival in the parish.

Upton Noble

Like most of the places with double-barrelled names, Upton Noble began as Upton in Saxon times. 'Noble' was the name of the Norman family to whom land was granted after the Norman Conquest. It is a tiny village with no more than 105 inhabitants, and with 100 fields in the parish. It stands just below the brow of a ridge, and looks across a glorious wide valley to the long line of Kingsettle Hill crowned by King Alfred's tower. There is always a wind blowing here. In a good mood one calls it bracing; in a bad mood something worse. At any rate, people live to a great age here, often well into their nineties.

It is not a pretty village, but it has a plain-faced, honest look. We are fortunate to live in 'stone country', so all the older houses, many of them centuries old are solid and thick-walled, built of 'shell' limestone, warm in colour. We marvel to see fossils in our house walls, remembering that the stone was formed millions of years ago below the sea. Several of the six farms have fields named 'Quarfield' or 'Quarryfield', where there was a small quarry which provided the stone for the farmhouse and outbuildings.

Although small, ours is a real village. It has a tiny, ancient church, with traces of Saxon and Norman, and a Mass Dial on the outer wall which announced the time of the service to the pre-Reformation congregation. The church is lovingly tended and decorated with flowers by a rota of village ladies. We have, too, a school which serves five villages, replacing the old handsome stonebuilt village school. This, after much energetic fund-raising was purchased from the County Council in 1979.

One claim to distinction is the Pound, no longer needed for straying animals, its original use, but made into a charming little garden, to commemorate the Silver Jubilees of King George V and Queen Elizabeth II.

Walton

Walton is an extremely ancient settlement dating back to Saxon times. Its name means 'a settlement of British Serfs' or 'a settlement in a wood' and is mentioned in the Domesday Book, at one time being part of the land under control of the monks in Glastonbury Abbey. Practically the whole of Walton was bought by Sir John Thynne in the 1530s, of whom the present Marquis of Bath is a direct descendant. Some 400 years later, on the 14th July 1939, a unique event in Somerset history occurred, the day an almost entire village came under the auctioneer's hammer. Divided into 137 lots, 34 farms and small holdings, 42 houses and cottages and one inn, together sold for the princely sum of £61,665 – less than the selling price of the last house completed in the village.

The post-war years have seen great changes in the parish, with nine working farms no longer existing as such, and the agricultural worker an almost extinct species; the remaining farms being worked by the owners and their families. Opportunities in other trades have opened up with two garages, a vehicle body repair shop and an engineering works, which began life in the old Walton estate carpenter's shop in 1953.

Many varied hobbies and pastimes must exist in a population of around 800. One must be a fondness for gardening which stirs much of the community each spring, but the long back garden with a pig fattening in the sty (probably the reason for Walton being rather derisively known as 'Pigtown' in parts of the county) have long vanished. With land prices at a premium, where once one farmhouse stood, there are six small terraced houses with equally small gardens. More unusual is the recently retired man with an extensive model railway system filling a whole room of his house. He keeps this pretty quiet, lest all the small boys of the parish beat a path to his door! Boys of 8 to 80 would delight in the model steam traction engines built by Mr Stone and his son, Bill.

The school, two village stores and post office, two pubs, the parish church, sited it is said at the centre of Somerset, and the Methodist church provide the meeting places essential to village life. News reaches the parish boundaries long before the local journal; mainly not as gossip but with genuine interest and concern.

Wambrook 🐏

Wambrook is an unspoilt Somerset village and one lady has vivid memories of visiting her relations at the smithy there in years gone by.

'What a welcome awaited us, the dogs and cats creating a hullabaloo, and then my Aunt Ellen and my cousin Edna, about my age, running out to greet us! We didn't dare disturb my Uncle Jack – he was a terrifying, very important man, with the roaring fire and bellows going for a backdrop. Into the old familiar parlour (having gone through the very cool and rather dark post office) and the savoury smell of a big baking tin of jointed rabbit stew, or for choice, a tin of real butchers' sausages.

After a brief rest, my cousin and I would set out down the road, past the school, the church, over a ford, round the corner and down the lane to a farm and a group of cottages. At the farm we collected a can of milk and also some delicious toffees or fruit sweets – they kept a few jars of each for sale. We then kept on the track which led us back to the smithy, a lovely way, involving crossing stepping-stones over a brook, and a winding track through clumps of wild orchids and kingcups. It was there that I saw my first kingfisher and also huge dragonflies about four inches long.

Back through the upper field then, waist high in bracken, to the smithy, with what remained of the milk!'

Wambrook has lost none of its charm and magic. The smithy is now gone, the school is the village hall and of course the ford is covered in. However, the lovely walk through the field with the brook is still there, and is unchanged.

Wanstrow 🐏

Wanstrow (Wandel's Tree) is a main road village on the eastern slope of the Mendips, where the Nunney brook rises. The main road was built by the Bruton Turnpike Trust around 1810, and the old road still wanders around the village. Gone are brickyard and station, but heavy loads of stone still run down from the Merehead Quarry, over the East Somerset Line.

Watchet 🐚

The village grew and developed 'below the Kirk, below the Hill, below the Lighthouse Top' as Coleridge wrote in his *Rime of the Ancient Mariner*. From village to Urban District and back to Parish Council within the West Somerset District when boundaries were re-organised in 1974. Today the main industries are the St Regis Paper Mill and the commerce of the harbour. An unusual balance is maintained in the use of the harbour by the Shipping Companies and the Boat Owners' Association, and although at low water the expanse of mud may seem depressing, at high water, on a sunny day, our harbour presents a delightful mixture of commerce and pleasure to say nothing of the serious business of fishing, with rod and line from the pier, with drop net for prawns, from boats for conger, cod and skate and even with a net for crabs from the slipway.

Lords of the Manor of Watchet are the Wyndham Family whose home is in the neighbouring village of Williton. Their family chapel is in Watchet's parish church, St Decuman's. This dedication commemorates a local saint and is the only church with that name in England. Nearby Kentsford Farm was their manor house. A famous legend tells of young Lady Florence Wyndham who had died and been buried at St Decuman's. She was buried with costly jewels and rings on her fingers and, according to legend, the greedy sexton opened her coffin that night, and, not satisfied with 'easy pickings', attempted to file a ring from her finger. Blood flowed and the Mistress of Kentsford sat up!! The sexton fled, the Lady left the vault and walked home to Kentsford. Later, she gave birth to twin sons and the carving on a bench-end in nearby Sampford Brett church is reputed to be of Lady Wyndham and her two sons.

The Court Room at Kentsford was the meeting place of the Court Leet, and even today the Court Leet is held in Watchet with the Steward of the Wyndham estate presiding and a traditional meal of Michaelmas goose, walnuts and rum punch, made from a secret recipe, is served. Port Reeve, Petty Constable, bread weighers, ale tasters, street keeper and an active town crier, are still appointed.

One of the privately-owned Steam Railways runs through Watchet, from Minehead to Bishop's Lydeard. There are areas of Outstanding Natural Beauty on the Quantocks and walks through lovely countryside, often with sea views on one hand.

Weare 🦋

Romans and Saxons, free men and slaves, English and Norman, pilgrims, travellers and tourists have all passed through Lower Weare on the Bridgwater Road. Some have paused but few, if any of them, turn off to find the quieter twin village of Upper Weare clustered round the little church.

Small though it is, it is a compendium of the centuries. Its Norman font, older than the present building, was made for the earlier simple church on the site, but the merchant, John Bedbere, whose brass effigy shows his well-filled purse, probably worshipped in the newly erected edifice at the end of the 15th century. The pulpit is Jacobean, the altar table is a Jacobean chest which was installed about a hundred years ago. The carved choir stalls are modern, the fine workmanship illustrating the life of St Gregory, the church's Patron Saint.

Outside the church stands the Butter Cross, the shaft dating from about 1350, and beside the church is the old Church Room, at one time the village schoolroom. Here boys and girls, often wearing starched white pinafores, were all taught in the one room. They had no playground, and if they were thirsty, they drank from the waterfall from the old vicarage garden, cupping the water in their hands. About 1896, the Luttrell family gave the land for the present school, which was enlarged in 1960. It also now has an excellent unit for children who have partial hearing and speech impediments.

In the 19th century there was a flourishing brickworks in Lower Weare. Mr Day was a brick, tile and drainpipe manufacturer, and lived in Brickworks House, next to the clay pit from where the clay was dug for the handmade bricks. The old clay pit eventually became the attractive lake and gardens of Ambleside, near to the Lamb at Weare pub.

The present bridge over the river Axe is not very old either, dating from 1928. The previous bridge had rings to tie up boats. The river now is hardly more than a stream, but in medieval times it was a busy thoroughfare all the way from the coast at Uphill to Glastonbury and the abbey there. It is hard to imagine nowadays, with a protective sea wall and so much drainage, how the tide can have rolled in, and how storms can have flooded the countryside.

Wedmore 🦢

In the year AD 878 King Alfred made peace at Wedmore with Guthrum the Dane. Since then no figure of national fame has touched the village; but two local inhabitants have left their own particular marks. One was a 17th century doctor, the other a Victorian businessman. The buildings they put up in the village survive today, as a reminder of their influence.

Porch House, at the west end of Wedmore, takes its name from the porch room, supported on two pillars, that projects over the front entrance. It was the home of the farming Westover family from the 1400s to 1766.

In 1643 John Westover was born, son of John Westover, surgeon. Of Dr John the elder, only his salutary epitaph, 'Repent, for doctors dye', survives. Dr John the younger continued to run the family farm and his father's practice, and of him much more is known. From 1685 to 1700 he kept a journal in which he wrote his accounts in broad 'Zummerset'. Farming activities are intermixed with the accounts of his patients, with details of their illnesses, remedies and cures.

Built in 1830, Tonkin's emporium was once the largest fashion store in rural Somerset

169

The second building stands in the centre of the village at the junction of Church Street with The Borough. It is large and imposing, and consists of a house and three-storey shop. This ornate building in Italianate style was put up by John Tonkin about 1830. John Tonkin, a native of Cornwall, settled in Wedmore and prospered. He started a brick and tile works, and eventually built his house and shop using his own bricks and tiles. The tiles were of a special 'fish tail' design produced exclusively for this building.

In its heyday, the shop became the largest fashion emporium in rural Somerset. John Tonkin and his wife Elizabeth lived in the adjoining house with their household staff. Mrs Tonkin used to travel to London to acquire the latest fashions and materials – quite a demanding journey in the mid 1800s.

Nowadays, Dr Westover has been superseded by a small health centre, while Tonkin's shop has become the village chemist, where patients get their prescriptions made up in what was the office and savings bank. The high fashion business continues just a few steps away in The Borough. Ladies still come from all over Somerset and beyond, to browse and buy. While they decide, they can take light refreshment, as they could over 150 years ago. The pioneering enterprise of the two Johns continues still, in Wedmore today.

West Bagborough

The parish of Bagborough is not only the straggling village on the south of the Quantock Hills; it extends over an area of hillside, farms, woodlands, moorland and circles. Will's Neck, the highest point of the Quantocks is the ancient site of the beacons which are still lit for festive occasions, as they were for the marriage of the Prince and Princess of Wales.

During the 14th century, the village was infected by the dreadful plague 'The Black Death' and the population was reduced to under 100 people. They decided to move away from the infection and built thatched cottages of cob ½ mile or so from the church and the old village. A number of these cottages still remain. The Rising Sun at the foot of Stout Lane is one and it is interesting that until about 1916, when it was sold, it was known as The Shepherd's Crook, and home brewed beer was produced by the owner Mr Rich. Until recently many of the older men still called it 'The Crook'.

Bagborough was a self-sufficient village. Every cottage had a small garden with a pig, a spinning wheel for the spinning of wool from the sheep that roamed over the hills, then woven into fabric for their clothes. Little girls from a very young age learnt to knit and weave and every small boy worked in the fields. The village has had a shop owned by the same family for about 100 years, where bread was baked by the baker, Marcus Sealey. Near at hand was the forge where tools of all sorts were made and the wheelwright worked with the smith to make waggons. He also made the cradles and coffins for the people of Bagborough.

West Buckland ✆

The village of West Buckland lies to the south of the A38 between the market town of Taunton and Wellington, in the Vale of Taunton Deane. The written history of West Buckland begins with a 10th century charter.

The church of St Mary dominates the village, standing on a knoll overlooking the M5 motorway, and across beautiful countryside to Wellington, some 2 miles distant. The traveller returning home during hours of darkness cannot fail to be gladdened by the sight of its floodlit tower. A visit to this cosy little church with its friendly atmosphere reveals a Norman font with (possibly) 15th century carvings, a fine rood loft staircase and a 100 year old renovated organ recently installed, having been bought from a church at Marlow.

Nestling at the foot of the hills is a most interesting old manor house, Gerbestone Manor, home of the Fox family, whose woollen mills in the town of Wellington have provided the local people with work for so many years. The house is basically 16th century, carefully restored by the present owners in 1924 after many years of decay. There is evidence however that part of the present house was built by John de Gerebert, High Sheriff of Somerset, in the 12th century.

The parish consists of first class farming land, mainly dairy and arable. Much of the land to the south of the village was parkland, belonging to the bishops of the diocese, until the year 1840. Many properties bear witness to this with such names as Park Farm, Park Bridge, Park Mead, Great Park etc. Several farms retain old family names such as Giffords, Barbers, Cades and Hopkins, among many others.

But probably the biggest changes in the village itself have occurred in the last 25 years. Many new houses and bungalows have been built, mainly on two estates, Dyers Estate and Church Drive.

West Buckland still retains its village school, taking at the present time 46 pupils from 5 to 11 years. This Board school, built in 1882 replaced the old church house school, the remains of which can be found on the right hand side of the path leading to the church, which is mentioned in 1603. There are two pubs, the Crown in the village itself and the interesting old Blackbird Inn on the A38, the old turnpike road. The parish can also boast two nurseries specialising in chrysanthemums, a nursing home for the elderly and two garages, both on the main road. The village shop and post office is a family run business serving the needs of a community where a bus service is almost non-existent.

Westbury-sub-Mendip

The village of Westbury-sub-Mendip (population 791 in 1985) lies at the foot of the southern slopes of the Mendip Hills and enjoys panoramic views over the moors to Glastonbury Tor nine miles away, and far beyond. It is situated on the busy A371 road, roughly halfway between Wells and Cheddar, and although recent years have seen an increase in the erection of new houses, some of the older dwellings are listed buildings – each with its own particular character and style. This makes Westbury a very interesting village to explore leisurely – preferably on foot.

Probably the first thing that catches the visitor's eye is the early 15th century stone cross which forms the hub of the village, situated close to Westbury's own pottery, the post office, the village school (built in 1860 and now having a roll of 80 pupils), and, of course, the church.

The church is dedicated to St Lawrence and goes back to Norman times. Like the majority of churches, it underwent a great deal of restoration in the late 19th century when the tower was rebuilt and the bells re-cast. The large, gnarled yew tree in the churchyard is reputed to be 800 years old and nearby a plot of ground (still not used for burials) marks the site of an old plague pit.

Every Spring Bank Holiday Monday, the Westbury Inn is the focal point for an almost unique gathering, for this is where Westbury Friendly Society meet after their annual march through the village, wearing statutory blue sashes and carrying their historical spears and banners. The Friendly Society dates back to 1771 and only two other Somerset Friendly Societies are still in existence. Celebrations continue with a

The fifteenth century village cross at Westbury-sub-Mendip

church service and an afternoon fête which is held on the lawns of Court House Farm.

The somewhat incongruous building set high on the top of the Mendips pinpoints Westbury Quarry. In 1969, quarrymen discovered some rhinoceros bones, and since then Westbury quarry has become world famous for the rich variety of fossiliferous animal remains found in the deposits filling a former cave.

On the same hill, just above Westbury, and accessible by a path known as the 'Coffin Track', lies the deserted village of Ramspit which was mentioned in the Bishop's old records of 1464. Although all that remains of Ramspit is four or five house platforms, the stunning views make it well worth the effort of walking there.

West Coker 🦢

The name Coker or Cocre is derived from the old English cucra meaning 'crooked stream' and there are plenty of those here. It is as Cocre that the village appears in the Domesday Book.

The church of St Martin of Tours has stood on this site since the 13th century and still retains two horn windows in the semi-circular stair turret. Glass would have been a luxury in the Middle Ages. The growing of hemp and flax and the manufacture of yarn was already common in this part of Somerset and hemp tithes were paid to the rector in 1309. This industry continued for many hundreds of years all around this area.

By the middle of the 17th century local canvas was in great demand, being whiter than canvas from other parts of the country and being supplied to the Navy for sails. By the time of Trafalgar the term Coker Canvas was in common use and in 1813 records state 'that the best kind of canvas now in use in the Navy is Coker Canvas'. Was Coker Canvas in fact used on Admiral Nelson's *Victory*? Local people like to think so.

As steam took over from sail in our ships, so the demand for sailcloth declined. Rope and twine continued to be made here until quite recently but that too has now declined to one manufacturer.

Some of the old names still remain – at one end of the village we have Hemplands and at the other, The Rope Walk and The Wash. Here the flax was washed and laid to bleach on the steep, ridged hills opposite Wash Cottage.

The tithe barn standing at the bottom of Pack Hollow is something of a puzzle. Bearing the date 1764 it was originally thatched and built on staddle stones. The window and door arches however appear to be 16th century and are reputed to have come from the old Shepton Mallett gaol. It would appear that farmers have always known a good bargain when they saw the chance!

West Coker seems to have suffered its biggest changes in the last 30 years. Not only has the rope and sailcloth industry disappeared but work on the land too has diminished and there is now only one working farm. But far from becoming a 'ghost' village there has been considerable building development bringing new people and new ideas.

West Huntspill 🌿

West Huntspill is a small village off the A38 in the north of the county. The older part of the village lies around the rectory and church, with its 15th century tower. In the 19th century a fire devastated the old church, destroying much of the interior, but a great deal of work was put into restoration and the church is still attractive today.

Vivid memories still abound of the floods which covered West Huntspill in December 1981. Having gone to bed on a Sunday evening, villagers were roused in the early hours by hurriedly spread flood warnings. Other properties were badly affected and parts of the village were cut off from the main road. There was devastation on the other side of Bleak Bridge. The sea, with no sea wall to halt its flow, just rampaged into Stretcholt.

Many people had to leave their homes and it was months before things returned to normal. The authorities built a new earth bank behind the old sea wall. The emergency committee formed then is still in existence and going strong.

West Lydford 🌿

The Rev John Collinson in the year 1790 wrote a short history of the villages in Somerset. Of West Lydford 'This place evidently obtained its name from its situation, there being in ancient times a broad ford here over the river Brue which runs through the village and has over it a good stone bridge near the church.'

Early spelling of Lydford is 'Liedford' meaning a torrent of water or where two streams converge. The country then, was low, flat and woody and the soil in general was a cold wet blue clay, mostly pasture and not very fertile. The number of houses in the village were 71 – 40 of which were farms. There were two grist mills, two public houses and the rest were cottages built from the local Keinton Stone with thatched roofs.

The church was originally a stone structure, consisting of a nave, chancel, a north aisle and a small tower at the west end contained five bells. The present church dedicated to St Peter (but the early maps say St Mary) was consecrated on the 14th day of August 1846 by Bishop Bagot.

In the churchyard there lies what was probably an interior monument taken from the earlier church, made of Bath stone, it is a figure in a position of repose. The arms are folded in prayer, but the legs which are usually crossed or straight are placed away from each other, suggesting that the memorial is one of a Crusader. The stone is in such a perished state it is impossible to discern either a name or date but it is thought to be either 10th or 11th century. Legend still persists however, that a man who lived at King-O-Mill wished to be buried where his arrow fell, so facing the east he stood, pulled his bow, the arrow fell half a mile away in the centre of West Lydford churchyard where now lies the monument.

The two mills mentioned in Collinson's History are no longer in use. One is known as the Old Mill and the other as King-O-Mill. Legend says that this mill is King Afred's Mill and here the flour with which he made the burnt cake was ground. The cakes were burnt at Athelney some 15 miles west of King-O-Mill.

Both these mills are connected by a stream of water; we believe that St Dunstan who started the milling industry in Somerset made this connection for it has been written that 'he started a stream from the river where again the river joins'. This is certainly the course of the millstream through West Lydford.

West Monkton ❧

A charter dated AD 682 was granted by King Centwine giving the abbot of Glastonbury certain lands including Quantock Wood, now known as West Monkton. It has been an area of landowners, tenant farmers, craftsmen and tradesmen.

In 1872 the manor became the property of Viscount Portman. There were 5 commons in the parish, a gravel pit, a parish quarry, 3 pounds for straying stock, 2 groups of houses for the infirm and poor, 3 buildings used for schools, 3 blacksmith's shops and 3 inns.

The parish is very large, beginning at the Quantock hills and extending on the south east nearly into Taunton.

The 15th century church stands very high on the hill and can be seen for miles around. There are traces of a Saxon church on the present site. It has 6 bells, a very ancient clock, and the barrel roof, 36 feet high, constructed in 1450 is very interesting. In the churchyard stand the stocks and whipping post, covered with a roof to preserve them.

Four almshouses under one roof, known as the Spital Almshouses, provide accommodation for elderly ladies of the parish who were once housed in the ancient Leper Hospital which was within the parish boundary. This building was rebuilt in the 16th century and is now restored, as the headquarters of the Somerset Rural Community Council. Records of this charity date back to the 12th century. It is still administered today by the Rector and representatives of the parish.

Corn mills, situated on the river bank, grinding corn into flour, were in existence for centuries until destroyed by fire in 1914. The canal brought coal on barges from Bridgwater to unload at the wharf, now St Quintins Guest House, to be taken by horse and cart to supply the country people. Along the canal bank was a sawmill, and the name Tanpits Farm suggests that tanning was carried on.

With the continuing growth of the village the small village hall was not adequate to house audiences at various events. A new village hall was built, entirely through voluntary effort and is well used by parishioners and outside organisations.

West Pennard 🌿

The name of West Pennard describes the village and gives a clue to its history. The Welsh words penn (a hill) and ardd (high) describe the site on the side of a hill. Over 500 years ago the church was built and the village grew up around it. The parish church is one of the most beautiful in Somerset, built in the perpendicular style. Set into the hillside on its slightly sloping site, you really do walk 'up' the aisle.

West Pennard is made up of five rural hamlets, mainly family farms producing milk, cheese and cider. They all got together in 1887 to produce the celebrated West Pennard cheese which was made from milk from every farm in the village. This was taken to London to be presented to Queen Victoria on the occasion of her Jubilee. It travelled to the city by horse and waggon with many unscheduled stops on the way for refreshment and many unofficial 'viewings of the cheese' which must have offended Her Majesty as the gift was refused on the grounds of so many people seeing it on its journey to her. The cheese duly arrived back to the village, rather the worse for its long journeying; it ended its days sadly in a barn where it eventually became a meal for the mice! To this day a replica of the cheese follower used in its making – with the Royal Coat of Arms – can be seen mounted on the wall of the village hall.

The old village was of traditional cottages and farmhouses, built of local stone with pantiled roofs. Since the Second World War modern houses have grown up making a mixture of both old and new, as with the

V.C. Primary School, blending the old original classrooms, including the village pump in the playground, with the very modern additions to cater for the many extra pupils from the surrounding villages.

Our community has grown also, with many new faces and our sturdy village hall acts as a centre from which so many social activities take place.

Westonzoyland ✍️

Westonzoyland (or Weston Zoyland) is built on one of three sand bars (or zoys, in the old dialect), on the flood plain of the low-lying area known as the Somerset Levels, north west of the ancient port of Glastonbury. The village is dominated by the 100 foot tower of the church of St Mary the Virgin.

Rebel prisoners, many recruited locally, were incarcerated in the church by the Royalist army following the Battle of Sedgemoor, the last battle on English soil, fought between the troops of the rebellious Duke of Monmouth and James II. It took place to the north-west of the village on 6th July 1685. Follow the signposts and walk alongside Bussex Rhine to the battleground. Both the battle site and the church lend themselves to the bleak reality the combatants must have faced that cold, misty dawn.

Memories of a more recent war will be stirred by the concrete runways to the south-east of the village. During the Second World War the airfield was extended, concrete runways and buildings for men and machines were built and British and American aircraft flew from here. In 1943 the Second Tactical Airforce practiced with gliders and paratroops for D-Day and in 1944 the USAAF 101st Airborne Division trained here before flying to Normandy. The airfield was finally closed for military purposes in 1958. Peaceful flying continues.

South-west of the village down lanes scented, in summer, with the aroma of meadowsweet can be found the Moreland Farm Pumping Station. This was the earliest steam pumping station on the Somerset Levels. Built in 1830 it worked until 1951 when it was replaced by a new diesel pumping engine in a separate building. A group of local enthusiasts have formed a charitable trust, and, operating with volunteer labour, have restored the old station and its equipment to 'steaming condition'. It is open to the public 'on steam', for several days throughout the year. During its working life the pumping engine drained 2,000 acres of the

178

Othery, Weston Zoyland and Middlezoy area of the Somerset Levels. Without the engine the land would frequently have been flooded, the three villages becoming islands in the floodwaters. The water was pumped into the river Parrett.

The modern village has expanded by the introduction of new estates and the life of the once typical moorland village is being quickened and a thriving community spirit is being engendered. It now boasts its power in many sports, cricket, football, squash etc at its Community Centre.

Whatley & Chantry

There has been a settlement at Whatley at least since Roman times. In AD 940 the manor was granted to the monks of Glastonbury. Now Whatley is a small village, dominated by the tower of the Norman church. To the north of the village is a large, working quarry.

Everything grows at Keeper's Cottage, Whatley – stately rows of beans and vegetables, flowers along walks shaded by bountifully bearing fruit trees, above all a special tree 25 feet tall, noted for its exceptionally heavy crop of apples.

Its story began in 1941 when Alice visited a friend and was presented with a lovely large apple. The colour was inviting – a lemon tinge merging with burnished speckled orange. At home, Alice dropped the apple core in a pot of geraniums outside the kitchen window, forgetting all about it. Next spring some tiny seedlings came up in the geranium pot. These were planted out and they grew into sizeable trees and bore a variety of apples. Only one, though, was orange and lemon-shaded, tasting somewhat of Cox's Orange Pippin. Now every Christmas privileged friends of Alice receive delicious parcels of apples – so far unnamed, but known to friends as 'Alice's Apples'!

At neighbouring Chantry in the 19th century, James Fussell, the ironmaster, built himself a mansion, complete with landscaped grounds and lake. The family later gave the small village a church and a school.

Williton

There is no clear, accepted derivation of the name Williton, the most popular one is Willet-tun, 'the place on the river Willit'. The village stands on what must always have been a natural crossroad with roads south, east and west converging in the main street of Williton.

We have only one 'famous' historical person to boast about, Reginald Fitz-Urse, one of the four knights who murdered Thomas a Becket. The Fitz-Urse family were Lords of the Manor for quite some time. The building of a chapel-of-ease in the parish of St Decuman, Watchet, was part of the penance imposed on Fitz-Urse for the murder. There are few remains of the original building as Williton became a Parish in its own right in 1857 when most of the present church was built. Unusually in a Victorian church the style is not heavily Victorian Gothic and the pillars are round as they are in early Norman churches.

There were several farmhouses and their outbuildings erected between circa 1610 and 1630, all substantial houses, and some splendid barns are still in use. Orchard Mill also dates from this period, most of the machinery and the water wheel are still in situ and were in use until about 15 years ago when Mr Sutton the miller retired. The mill stones are still capable of being used to grind grain and the waterwheel has been restored by the tenants who have a rural museum and a restaurant on the site. Another local attraction is the West Somerset Railway.

This is a large pleasant village, the buildings spanning a long period of time, from the cottages near the church which are said to date from the 13th century through Tudor, Stuart and Georgian times to the present day. The Williton Hospital, about to be replaced by a new purpose-built hospital, is housed in part of a workhouse designed by Gilbert Scott who later designed Liverpool Cathedral. We also have a very splendid stone-built Victorian Police Station; in the wall in front of the Police Station there are the iron brackets that were used to tether cattle when there was a fortnightly market in the street.

Winsford 🐚

Two miles from Bridgetown lies the most attractive village of Winsford. Said to be 'the prettiest village on Exmoor', it derives its name from the ford over the Win Brook. Its most famous inhabitant was Ernest Bevin, born there in 1881 and educated at the village school. He became a Member of Parliament and after the Second World War became Foreign Secretary. Winsford still has a village school – recently the subject of threatened closure, but happily now allowed to continue to serve the surrounding villages.

The church was renovated in the 15th century, but retains some Norman features. The village centre has a number of thatched cottages and boasts a famous thatched inn – The Royal Oak – where many visitors come to stay and sleep in four poster beds! Opposite the inn is an ancient pack-horse bridge. Other famed inhabitants are a small gaggle of white geese who can frequently be seen holding up the traffic whilst they waddle in line astern across the road.

Winsham ✍

This village on the borders of Dorset and Somerset is known by the older folk as Winsum. It is a very compact village with many old buildings, including 8 thatched cottages still in use. One villager with long roots in the village remembers:

'Memories remain of my Grandfather Good, who in younger life, worked at the cloth factory, for which he used to collect folks' urine in the days of no flush toilets. This was used to soak cloth and the families who produced the most were given a length of cloth at Christmas, a real treat.

My grandfather was also Bell Captain. The bells were rung twice on Sundays and at six o'clock on Christmas and Easter mornings. He also wound the church clock at the same time each Saturday night; we still have the little stool he used.

The village Jubilee Hall, in the centre of Church Street, was given by Lord Bridport, who lived at Cricket St Thomas, the stones and timbers being taken from nearby fields and woods. In my father's time the hall was used for a reading room and during the last war as a school for evacuees.

The church goes back to the 13th century. Winsham was once linked with Combe, sharing a vicar. The 15th century saw an increase in population and improvements were made to the church and the parish had its own vicar. On the north wall is the Tympanum, a wooden, painted picture of the Crucifixion. There is only one other such work in England.

Fry's Cocoa people, who lived at Cricket during the early 1900s, were kind to the local village folk, many of whom worked on the estate. My father was a gardener. He, as well as others, was left £10 when the master died. He would joke that if it had not been for that he would have been unable to get married.

The Village Cross is situated where five roads converge; once it was a meeting place for traders. Sadly the trough, with pump, is no more. We are lucky still to have the original village shop, now with the post office as part of it. After a hundred years only one inn remains, with traces of olden days.

However the countryside around seems much the same until one sees that the hedges are gone, meaning less wild life, such as the glow-worms, which were a welcome sight when we walked home from chapel, up those dark lanes. My grandfather would put one in his hat . . . such a beam from so small an insect!'

Witham Friary

It was here at Witham Priory that Henry II founded the first monastery for Carthusian monks in England, as an act of penance after the murder of Thomas a Becket in 1170. The village church is late 12th century and was built by the monks.

Over a hundred years ago the people of Witham believed in witchcraft! A well known character named Betty Ames had the reputation of being a witch, she was a tall woman who walked with a limp. She lived by herself in a thatched cottage at Upper Holt, and on the other side of the road lived a baker who kept a pony and trap. The poor baker was very unlucky, as pony after pony 'went wrong', and the blame was laid at Betty Ames' door.

Witham Friary still has its Friendly and Benevolent Society, the earliest recorded date of which is 1786. A celebration was held every Whit Tuesday, when the members marched behind a magnificent banner and a brass band, every member proudly wearing a rosette made of blue and white ribbon.

In 1943, when enemy planes were bombing Bristol every night, they would fly nose to tail over Witham and Gare Hill, drop their bombs on Bristol and fly back the same way. During one of these raids, an aircraft jettisoned its bombs near Gare Hill, and then crashed into the woods after being shot down by the RAF. The woods were so dense that it was several years after the war before a woodman stumbled on the skeleton wearing the uniform of a German airman. Altogether five enemy planes were shot down in this area by the RAF.

Withycombe

This pretty village, set amongst some of the most beautiful scenery in Somerset, is mentioned in the Domesday Book and at one time was vested in the family of Dunster Castle. It derives its name from the Anglo-Saxon 'Withig' meaning a willow, withy or osier, and combe – a valley, thus the Valley of Willows.

The church, which is early 13th century and dedicated to St Nicholas has many interesting features. It has a square embattled tower containing four bells which are still rung, a fine Norman font and a Holy Water stoop in the porch. It also has a chalice reputed to be Elizabethan. Probably the churchyard is best known as it contains the grave of the 'Witch of Withycombe'. This lady whose name was Joane Carne, was three times married and lived in the manor house at Sandhill. She died in 1612 and was thought by many people to have been a witch and to have 'done away' with her three husbands and to have haunted Sandhill since her death. After her funeral when the mourners returned to Sandhill, her ghost was seen frying eggs and bacon in readiness for their return. To the discomfort of the inhabitants of Sandhill, she continued to haunt the house until her unquiet spirit was laid, in the manner of those times, by seven parsons with bell, book and candle in a pond on Sandhill Farm, from which she is reputed to take a cock's stride in the direction of Sandhill, once a year; we do not know what will happen when her journey ends.

Still in the parish of Withycombe lies Rodhuish, a tiny hamlet boasting of being recorded in the Domesday Book and to be of ancient foundation. The name is interesting because in Domesday Book it is called Radehewis and signifies the residence or dwelling place of the Radmen or judge. Radmen were the origin of the present jury and had to pass an examination in the knowledge of their profession, a chief judge would have a council consisting of several members called Radmen or counsellors. The church of Rodhuish is of ancient foundation, but stands firm and well used to this day and is lit only by candle-light which restricts services to mornings in the winter.

Wiveliscombe 🍃

Wiveliscombe (which name is said to be derived from the English chief called Wifela or Wyfel, who took possession of the combe in Anglo-Saxon times), is pleasantly situated at the foot of the Brendon Hills, 11 miles from Taunton, 6 miles north-west of Wellington and but 5 miles from the Devon boundary.

In the 1880s Wiveliscombe was a lively, prosperous place. The major employers of the area were the well known Hancock family. Their famous brewery, founded in 1807 and sited in Golden Hill, was the largest brewery in the South West by the 1880s and produced 200,000 gallons of beer per annum. Their equally famous cider factory was opened in the early 1900s in Golden Hill and the Hancock family also ran a large linen/draper's shop and a bank in Wivey.

Sadly, by 1955 the Brewery was bought out by Ushers, followed soon by its closure when Watneys gained control. This was the close of a chapter for 'Wivey,' and many said that life would never be the same again.

In 1966 the railway line from Taunton to Barnstaple fell under the Beeching axe, and Wiveliscombe Station was closed. This marked the end of yet another chapter for Wivey. Shops began to close, the population began to change and Wiveliscombe gradually lost status from an urban to a rural, and finally to a parish council.

The emergence of the modern landscape has also brought changes. Three council estates have been built in addition to a block of flats built on the site of the old cider factory (which was razed to the ground by fire in 1969). Some small private housing developments have appeared, as well as a large comprehensive school, a modern health centre, and a relief road opened in 1980 for through traffic. The nearby attractively designed reservoirs of Clatworthy and Wimbleball, and the local Maundown Water Treatment Works also now form part of the local scene.

However, despite many changes over the century the picturesque square, the Georgian and many of the other older buildings and cottages remain. Wiveliscombe is still an ideal spot from which to explore the softly wooded Brendon Hills, dramatic Exmoor, and the Vale of Taunton.

Near to Wiveliscombe, the small village of Huish Champflower is set in deep valleys and green hills. Its church of St Peter is of interest, having some ancient glass which probably came from the ruined priory of Barlynch.

184

Wookey Hole 🐚

Wookey Hole is famed for its caves and its witch. It lies at the foot of the southern slope of the Mendip Hills, at the point where the river Axe emerges from the great caves which gave the village its name. The name has varied over the centuries and is probably derived from the Celtic wocob or ocob, meaning cave. The village owes its existence to the caves and the river, and has a long history of human habitation.

The most famous inhabitant of Wookey Hole is undoubtedly the Witch of Wookey, who has become the emblem of the village. This venerable lady is, in fact, a stalagmite, roughly in the shape of a hag-like woman. Legend tells of a crone living in the caves, tending her goats, and thought to be a witch. Naturally, she was blamed for all local mishaps, and a monk was sent from Glastonbury Abbey to deal with her. This he did by sprinkling her with Holy Water, which turned her to stone, as visitors to the caves can see to this day.

The Axe, flowing from the caves, fed by the rain falling on the Mendips, made Wookey Hole an obvious site for a water-mill. Records from 1656 mention Thomas Weare, paper maker of Wookey Hole. In 1848 the paper-mill was bought by the Hodgkinson family, who built the present mill, the church, the school, Wookey Hole Club (for the use of the villagers) and many houses to provide accommodation for their employees. This transformed a scattered settlement into a recognisable village. The building was done with locally quarried stone, giving the village its special character, not picturesque but solid and purposeful. The paper-mill is now part of the Wookey Hole Caves complex and paper is still made there by hand using traditional methods.

At Ebbor Gorge, near the caves, the Nature Conservancy Council manages a nature reserve, on ground given to the National Trust by one of the Hodgkinsons, in memory of Winston Churchill.

Apart from tourism there is little employment in the village. Some people keep up the tradition of paper-making, working at St Cuthbert's Mill in the nearby hamlet of Haybridge. Others travel to neighbouring towns for work. The children go to school in Wells. The village still supports a church, although the Methodist Chapel has been converted into a sculptor's home and studio. There is a shop/post office, a pub and Wookey Hole Club, and the village has a number of clubs, associations, bowling and skittles teams and the like. It is a friendly village, welcoming to newcomers, and quietly proud of its heritage.

Woolavington

No-one visiting this large and friendly village today could imagine the picture it would have presented only 60 years ago. It was a small, isolated rural community; the Levels flooded and were unusable all winter, and there was no bus service.

Woolavington was founded by a Saxon, one Hunlaf, at about the end of the 9th century. He found a strategic place, about a mile below the busy trading route built by the Romans and above the flood line of the Levels – useful for fishing and wood!

The church has a Norman door and although the exact date is not known, it must have been there by the end of the 12th century. It is at the centre of the old village and is the focal point for much activity.

Although life was hard and work long and arduous, the villagers enjoyed a lot of fun – mostly of their own making. The Fair, charter granted in 1777, was eagerly awaited on October 18th each year in the square. Horses were in Tapps Lane, sheep in the main road, cattle in the square. Naptha flares lighted the stalls.

Mrs Eliza Bastable, a local lady, sold her gingerbread and brown rock at all the fairs. She was a colossal lady and it was said she had to wear jerseys for stockings! Buried here in the churchyard, her coffin was 3 feet across. The last fair was in 1914.

Very few changes happened until 1940 when a new estate was built on Woolavington Hill to accommodate workers at the nearby Royal Ordnance Factory. A drain was constructed on the Levels to supply the factory with water. This turned the marshy levels into rich pasture land, available to farmers all the year round.

This was the turning point in the life of the village, from a maximum of 400 inhabitants before the war, in the next 25 years an extensive but controlled building plan, road improvements and other amenities turned it into a thriving place of some 3,000 people. Most of the farms have gone, but pleasant homes with pretty gardens have taken their place.

Hymerford House, East Coker

Index

190